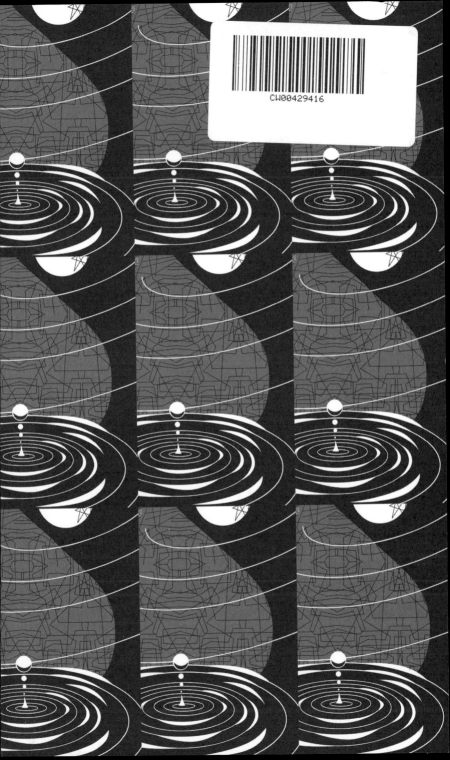

Thoughtful
Leadership

Thoughtful Leadership

A guide to leading with mind, body and soul

Fiona Buckland

Leaping Hare Press

First published in the UK and North America in 2021 by

Leaping Hare Press

An imprint of The Quarto Group
The Old Brewery, 6 Blundell Street, London N7 9BH, United Kingdom
T (0)20 7700 6700 **F** (0)20 7700 8066
www.QuartoKnows.com

British Library Cataloguing-in-Publication Data
A catalogue record for this book is available from the British Library

ISBN: 978-0-7112-6171-6

This book was conceived, designed and produced by

Leaping Hare Press

58 West Street, Brighton BN1 2RA, United Kingdom
Publisher RICHARD GREEN
Commissioning Editor MONICA PERDONI
Project Editor JOE HALLSWORTH
Designer GINNY ZEAL
Illustrator MELVYN EVANS

Printed in China

1 3 5 7 9 10 8 6 4 2

CONTENTS

INTRODUCTION

*We need good leaders. The issues we face
are too great and complex, the consequences of
thoughtless leadership too serious for us, for future
generations of all living beings, and for the planet.
A thoughtful leader takes responsibility for their world,
and brings forth their whole potential and the
potential of others for the greater good. Leadership is
about standing up, showing up and stepping up,
whether you want to take leadership of your own
life, hold or aspire to a leadership role in your
organization or community, lead your own projects,
lead through crisis, or seek to make political,
social or cultural change. The world is
calling. We need you.*

LEADERSHIP AS A SEARCH FOR MEANING

◆

We have a choice. We can choose to live our lives reacting to events, or we can choose how to respond, and can commit to living more meaningfully, making a difference for the good of the world.

WHEN I WAS A CHILD, I was told that when I died, Saint Peter would be waiting at the pearly gates with a book in which all my good and bad deeds on Earth would be recorded. If I was good, I might be granted entry to Heaven. If I was bad, the everlasting hellfire of damnation awaited. It was a useful way to persuade a small girl not to cheek her teachers. Although my belief in celestial gatekeepers has waned, I do know that one day will be my last, and as every day takes me closer to that point, certain questions become more urgent and important: 'What difference have I made? Have I lived this one precious life allowing its currents and squalls to carry me? Or have I checked my ship is yar, my shipmates ready and willing, and my compass set right? Have I placed my hands on the wheel and steered my life for the benefit of the world, knowing that whatever the elements throw at me, I will never lose my North Star?'

Leadership is above all a quest for meaning. I have the privilege of working as a leadership coach and facilitator, which I define as helping people make a conscious impact in their lives and the world, for the benefit of both. I'll tell you my

secret: I am a stealth soul worker. Potential clients may approach me asking for support to devise strategies, organize campaigns, give speeches, improve the performance of their teams, steer through crisis and change, have a better work/ life balance or lower stress and anxiety, but, as we work together, it becomes clear that these are gateway issues. What they seek at a deeper level is meaning, and standing up to take leadership is their path to living more fully and meaningfully.

To do this well requires deep connection with yourself, others and the world – connection which, I believe, many of us have lost because we live in internal and external environments that seem set up to separate us from ourselves, others and the world through distraction, avoidance and fear. At the fundamental level, I help people connect with themselves. They connect to their hearts to find out who they are, what's important to them, what they uniquely have to offer, and what they share with the rest of humanity. They connect to their souls, which reach for meaning and higher purpose in the knowledge that one day this life will be done, and all that will remain is the difference they made. Part of the leadership path is remembering, as much as learning. This book is aimed to show you some of the ways you can do this, and so become a good leader by becoming a thoughtful one, committed to lifelong self- and other-development, to release the potential in all of us for the sake of all living beings for generations going forward.

My Leadership Journey

The search for meaning and purpose through leadership is my own journey too. I didn't start out knowing that this would be how I made a difference in the world. For many years, I was an academic, obtaining degrees and awards, teaching and lecturing, and ending up as a Fulbright scholar with a doctorate in Performance Studies from New York University. I learned about the power of confidence, curiosity, listening and storytelling, as well as my responsibility towards those about whom this is written. But while I could read and even teach the most complicated theory, my own heart and the hearts of others remained an indecipherable text.

When I returned to the UK, I joined the then-new adventure of e-commerce. Corporate life excited me. We made decisions quickly, we were clear on what we were trying to do and why. It felt positively rock and roll to me, after the slower pace of academia. This was also where I had my first taste of managing teams, which – unprepared as I was – overwhelmed me with the challenge that was other people. Then I was poached by a large publisher, and I learned resilience, not just because of the demands of processes, accountability and targets, but also because when I was made redundant, I discovered how strong I was. When I subsequently became Managing Director of an independent publishing house, I brought with me a desire to develop and support my team, and to represent a mission to make cultural change.

I tell my clients, who may feel stuck, that their 'stuckness' is not a personal failing, or the opposite of growth. Stuckness is part of the process of growth, and of the quest for meaning. Sensing I wanted to make a change from publishing, but feeling lost, I saw a coach for the first time. With his help, I realigned around my values and purpose, rather than my skills and experience. It was transformational, and my next role was Head of Learning with a business focused on helping people develop emotional skills such as confidence, calm, resilience, entrepreneurial thinking and leadership. Despite loving the mission and work, I often sat in a mostly empty room crafting self-development classes, with loneliness rippling through me. When I had the opportunity to facilitate classes myself, my heart soared. I wanted to connect with people, to feel more directly that I was of service.

To do this well, I trained as a coach, and now work with individuals and groups, and facilitate workshops and leadership development programmes. My success since then has testified to the power of living my core values of love, growth and service. Each step of my journey has taught me something about my leadership story. I have thought a great deal about what success is, and this is it: to live with integrity, your inner life aligned with how you show up in the world. My drive is fueled, on one hand, from a satisfaction in seeing people make a difference in their own lives and in the world, and on the other, from a passionate belief that we need good leaders.

ABOUT THIS BOOK

You are on the hero's journey: from hearing the call to action that enticed you to pick this book up, to stepping over the threshold into the unknown, so you may return with gifts that will be of service to others. This is the leadership path, and you don't walk it once, you commit and re-commit to it every day.

I HAVE ORGANIZED THIS BOOK into five sections to reflect the path of leadership from internal to external work. Leadership is both being and doing. The first two chapters cover essential inner work: aligning with our authentic values and purpose, and managing our inner states. The third chapter explores how to authentically develop leadership range, so you have conscious choice how to show up in the world. Chapter four develops this outwards to your relationships with those you lead, and the final chapter expands into how we as leaders impact culture, and the future of leadership, looking at areas such as resilience, diversity, creativity, prospection and sustainability.

I stand on the shoulders of those who have come before me. I leave complex theory aside to focus on actionable ideas and practices, tested in the kitchen of coaching and facilitating leaders and leadership teams internationally. I look forward into the leadership we need, and have chosen practices that will continue to support thoughtful leadership.

I have seen how transformational change occurs over time when people integrate these practices into their everyday lives. In a short book, I can only cover so much, and my intention is to offer gateways you can walk through to find your own authentic way to deepen your learning and your leadership. A short bibliography is included at the end of the book.

Making Time for Leadership

The most important leadership practice is setting time aside for this work without interruptions. You need to make the time if you want to be a thoughtful leader. Carve time for self-reflection and to hone your leadership practices on a daily or weekly basis and hold boundaries. Be your own gatekeeper and recruit others to assist. Resist the temptation to cram in another email. Thoughtful, effective leadership isn't about getting everything done, but getting the right things done, and making time to nourish your own leadership isn't optional. Many leaders have coaches to help them do this. You may not have your own coach, but you do have this book, and inside it an invitation to practise the ideas and exercises within. You cannot be a good leader without working at it.

The Three Cs

I begin my workshops with three 'Cs' – compassion, courage and committment – and I offer them to you to create the framework in which I encourage you to approach this work.

First, Compassion: we judge ourselves too harshly. We'll forget things, screw up and sometimes fail. That's part of the process, and learning how to be more compassionate towards ourselves and others is an essential leadership practice.

Second, Courage: we can judge ourselves from a place of scarcity – 'I am less than a good leader' – rather than credit ourselves with our courage for trying. As US president Theodore Roosevelt wrote:

The credit belongs to the man who is actually in the arena, whose face is marred by dust and sweat and blood, who knows the great enthusiasms, the great devotions, and spends himself in a worthy cause; who at best, if he wins, knows the thrills of high achievement, and, if he fails, at least fails daring greatly, so that his place shall never be with those cold and timid souls who know neither victory or defeat.

We talk about 'hard' and 'soft' skills, but the so-called soft skills are incredibly hard because of the emotional work they demand of us, and that work is fundamentally the work of leadership.

Finally, Commitment: change won't come from reading the book, but from integrating many of these practices into your everyday life. You will find what works for you, so experiment, and don't give up. This is how you will develop as a thoughtful leader.

The Need for Thoughtful Leadership

You stand on a threshold now, and my aim for this book is that it helps you over it into the thoughtful leadership our times demand. We face local and global issues, for instance, inequality, climate change and healthcare crises. We need good leadership. The ones who make a positive difference are thoughtful leaders: leaders who speak with authenticity, empathy, compassion, clarity and wisdom; who are transparent and trustworthy; who do not see themselves as separate; and who appeal to our better natures, empowering us, even as they ask us to move out of our own comfort zone and change.

The mindset of thoughtful leadership is not confined to an elite few. It's a journey we all need to take. It holds the promise of a parallel process of self-development and co-creating a more sustainable world built on shared humanity, connection, awareness and responsibility.

We have to learn and adapt fast, and radically. Life demands our growth. We cannot stay children, imagining that someone else is coming to save us. Thoughtful leadership is the path of emotional maturity: of responsiveness, rather than reactiveness, and of responsibility, rather than blame. You are not alone on the path. We have important and, in some ways, painful choices to make, for we cannot continue as we have been. Thank you for standing up.

CHAPTER ONE

WHY DO YOU WANT TO LEAD?

*You opened this book because you want to
take leadership. Something stirs within your heart,
and simultaneously calls to you from the world.
What bridges them is your leadership path: a lifelong
series of invitations to realize the potential in yourself
and others, for the good of the world. My first
invitation is to connect authentically with yourself.
Let's begin.*

THE FIRST QUESTION

◆

A leader doesn't need to have all the answers. A leader explores questions: what, how, who, when, and above them all, why. When you live your why, you live the question of your purpose.

A CLIENT COMES TO ME for leadership coaching. They might already be an established leader, or someone taking their first steps, or they could want to develop more self-leadership. I ask this question first: 'Why do you want to lead?' Often, this evokes a slightly startled response: perhaps the client raises their eyes skyward and shifts in their seat, as if trying to wriggle free of something uncomfortable. It becomes clear they haven't given much thought to this question. They might talk fluently, if slightly automatically, about how important leadership is as a function of their life, business, organization, project or movement, but they don't seem to be clear why they want to lead. I open the question out:

- Why is it good that *you* lead?
- Why is it good for the people that you lead?
- Why is it good for your organization or community?
- Why is it good for the leaders who come after you?

If you can't answer these questions yet, don't judge yourself. If you have answers, remain open to discover more. The poet Rainer Maria Rilke wrote to a young writer who sought his advice:

'Be patient toward all that is unsolved in your heart and try to love the questions themselves, like locked rooms and like books that are now written in a very foreign tongue. Do not now seek the answers [...] Live the questions now. Perhaps you will then gradually, without noticing it, live along some distant day into the answer.'

We will revisit these questions at the end of this chapter, and I recommend you return to them on every step on your leadership path.

Authentic Leadership

Close your eyes and bring to mind someone you consider to be a great leader. What do you notice about them? Are they standing on a podium addressing a rapt crowd, or facing down a line of police? Chances are you measure your own leadership style against others. How do you feel about your leadership abilities compared with the charisma of Nelson Mandela, the moral power of Greta Thunberg, the vision of Steve Jobs, the gravity of Angela Merkel, the brainpower of Bill Gates, or the fearlessness of Malala Yousafzai?

We are bombarded with cultural messages about what leadership looks like, which generate conscious or unconscious pressure to adopt certain styles or skills – eloquence, for instance, or extroversion. Some doubt they have the right stuff to lead because they internalize such messages, and discount what they have to offer. Others try to wear an

inauthentic costume of what they think leadership looks like. But thoughtful leadership is about being yourself, the person you were always meant to be.

When any of us live out of alignment with our true selves, we catalyze suffering and blind spots. The impact zone of this can be great for leaders, because they cast a long and deep shadow. A leader needs integrity. Dissonance between who we are and how we lead, and between what we say and how we act, has an outsized effect on those around us. People disengage from a leader who cannot walk their talk. Leadership is conveyed both in our actions and our way of being. When you say that you are approachable and open, but avoid making eye contact, keep your door permanently closed, or talk over other people, then the thread of trust between you and others becomes brittle and shatters. You might not notice it breaking, yet wonder why projects don't run well, and people leave. Unfortunately, some leaders' is to blame more, and tolerate less. They become the bullies they might never have intended to be, and sadly, this coercive style is one of those unhelpful leadership templates our culture propagates, despite burgeoning evidence of its negative consequences and ineffectiveness over the long-term.

If you live an inauthentic life, you commit an act of violence upon yourself, and spread toxic stress deeply and widely. When you mindfully align with your whole self, you tap into your authentic power. You feel confident taking a

True & False Self

We all wear a public face. As we grew up, we learned to craft them to be successful socially and professionally. We show different sides of ourselves to lovers and work colleagues, for instance. Depending on the messages we received and understood as a child, many of us also learned not to show vulnerability. We have a very human tendency to want to protect our true selves to avoid feeling hurt, but the downside is that we miss deep connection with others. Over time, we might identify with the 'false self', and feel drained from maintaining a façade. The false self isn't bad – in fact it served you, as you learned to adapt successfully to your environment. Good self-leadership means being aware of both the false and the true self, and asks us to develop conscious ownership and mastery over them. A senior executive in a world-leading organization was asked in a public meeting what his biggest mistake was: 'Not coming out sooner', he replied, showing his authentic whole self, and demonstrating the humanity we all share, no matter what our job titles.

stand on something you believe in, even if you are alone. Start your leadership journey by putting away comparisons and costumes, and align with your values and purpose, so that you know in your heart and soul why you want to lead.

YOUR STORY

---◆---

Your story holds the crucible from which your leadership purpose emerges. When you know your story, and communicate it, you mine the past to energize the present, and envision the future.

LEADERS DON'T APPEAR FROM NOWHERE. We all have a story, which contains the crucible of your desire to lead and the values by which you do so. The essence of leading with authenticity is knowing what you care about, and then doing your best to be true to your values and purpose. To walk this talk, I'm going to tell you a part of my own story.

I experienced my first face-on-the-floor panic attack when I was forty-two. In the previous years, relationships ended, my brother became critically ill, I suffered a severe depression, was made redundant, and left my home. Unconsciously, I reverted to my failsafe habits of work and taking care of everyone else to feel secure. But although I was pulling the old levers, the machinery wasn't responding. I had run out of road, and needed to find another way forward.

A good friend suggested therapy. The process couldn't promise to make me better, but it could make me different – if I chose to be. Yet I kept holding fast to a story of loss and abandonment through which I filtered my life experience. I couldn't conceive of any other possible story. The reason lay in an unconscious belief that was running my life. My mother

MINDFULNESS EXERCISE

YOUR STORY

Writing by hand or drawing helps accelerate personal growth through revealing important insights that can be difficult to access. Set aside time to do this without interruption or distraction.

1 Create a timeline of your life, in whichever way suits you. Some people like to draw a simple timeline from birth to the present; others draw a map of a river running through a changing landscape.

2 Once you have done this, sit back and take a look. Identify moments where you had a call-to-action in the form of a choice you made – perhaps a job you took, a relationship you began or ended, or somewhere you chose to live. Your choice might have been made during a personal crisis such as experiencing an illness, loss or redundancy, or a national or local one, such as a health crisis, political upheaval or community issue.

3 Note down what you decided to do or how you chose to respond, and the strengths, strategies, resources, insights and values you drew upon. How are they expressed and realized in your leadership? In what ways does your experience influence your leadership style/goals?

died when I was two, and I had been adopted. Somewhere in my child's understanding, I created the belief that I had caused my mother's death. Out of loyalty to her, and fear of a dreadful reckoning, I had lived my life convinced that I would die at the same age as her. Now, as that milestone drew closer, the internal alarm bells were ringing.

My call-to-action was not to seize the sword and step out into the world. With quiet and tender heroism, I first had to learn to listen to myself with compassion. Although painful at times, the suffering of living a divided life, disconnected from my whole self, was greater. I discovered that by accepting myself more, I could connect with an authentic inner source of wisdom, clarity, courage and love. I needed to take another leap of faith to leave working for others, to work in service of others through coaching, facilitating and writing. How I chose to deal with a crisis in my life reveals a great deal about my core values of growth, love, courage and service. We become the leaders we need.

YOUR VALUES

In the demands of leadership, it's easy to get lost. Values are your personal GPS or compass — an internal navigation system by which you can align yourself. When we align with our values, we feel energized and motivated, and we attract people to us who recognize our integrity and shine with the same values. When we are not aligned with our values, we generate dissonance, disengagement and demotivation in ourselves and those around us.

MOST OF US LIVE OUR LIVES following the scripts of others, often those of our families, work and cultures. When we step over the threshold into thoughtful leadership,

we stay mindful of the influence of scripts that are not ours, and instead we write our own. Although not bad or wrong, when we steer our lives with extrinsic motivations often elevated by our culture, such as earning money and achieving status, we are more short-term focused, less creative and may end up with a sense of emptiness. A word to the would-be-worthy: there is no moral judgment around values; affluence, achievement and status are values, but we need to check they are intrinsic ones, rather than empty vessels we feel should motivate us. When we choose to follow intrinsic motivations – those authentic values that motivate us from within – we are energized over the long-term, are more innovative and thoughtful, and feel more fulfilled. The best leaders are energized by intrinsic, authentic values: the codes and principles by which we want to live our lives and in which we believe deeply. The world needs leaders who are clear what they stand for, and what that looks like in everyday life. To uncover our values and principles, the only guidebook we need is our lived experience.

Values form the DNA of your leadership style and effec-tiveness. A value is not an interest like nature, nor a goal like travel. Dig deeper and once you unearth what's important to you about nature or travel, you'll hit your personal seam of values. For me, nature connects me to wonder and transcen-dence; travel ignites my values of exploration, learning and courage. For another person, nature might be important

A Coaching Story: The Authentic Leader

I once coached a politician who worked in an environment that brimmed with people with different educational backgrounds and career journeys than her own. When they debated the finer points of policy, she felt she didn't know enough to stand next to or at times against them, and was afflicted by Imposter Syndrome. When I led her through an exercise to uncover her authentic values, she gained conscious awareness that she was at essence heart-led. She valued connection, justice and supporting and mentoring others, especially women in politics. She realized she needed to act from her own values, to be herself rather than worrying she wasn't enough in comparison to others. Her anxiety decreased, her sense of her own power increased, and so did her leadership effect.

---

because they value the achievement of climbing peaks, and travel because they treasure family. By becoming curious about those experiences in which we feel energized, we can start to listen to what our lives tell us about our values.

Once you have identified what your values are, then you can ask yourself these questions:

- How am I honouring my values?
- How am I dishonouring my values?

- How might I do or be something in a way that honours my values?
- What are other people's values?
- What are our shared values?

Aspired Values

On any journey there are dangers. There are many values to which we might *aspire* as leaders, but are not authentic to us. For instance, I might say I value self-discipline; however, if you offered me a life without it, I'd probably take it. It's not a core value, more a learned, culturally sanctioned behaviour that has been useful to me. But if I could never be compassionate or connect with others – values which are integral and dear to me – I would walk away without a second thought. Without the opportunity to live and work by my values, I would be deeply unhappy and ill-serving.

On your leadership path, your *values-in-action*, rather than aspired values, are the compass that keeps you aligned with your inner self. This is why the exercise to uncover your values-in-action, included in this chapter, is based on your experience, rather than a list of values to tick off. When you need to make a decision, find a choice aligned with your values. Even if you need to do so reluctantly, you can honour your values not just in *what* you do, but in *how* you do it.

MINDFULNESS EXERCISE

YOUR VALUES-IN-ACTION

This exercise uncovers your authentic values-in-action. You will need a pen and paper and some time for yourself.

1 Visualize your perfect day: a day when you feel really alive, when you are in your full power, living your fullest potential. Be specific. This might not be a time when you are lying on a beach, it could be a day of crisis or challenge, when you are stepping up and feeling a sense of achievement. Write it down.

2 Get interested in the detail of this image. Where are you? What are you doing? What can you see, hear, touch, taste and smell? What are you wearing? Are you alone or are you with another person, or more than one? What is important to you about that relationship? How do you feel?

3 Mine your visualization by asking what is important to you about it. For instance, is it because you are *making a difference* in some way? Are you feeling energized because you feel a strong *connection* to someone? Write down a list of the values you uncover. The examples given here are intended to help, but resist the urge to pick them without starting with your peak experience.

4 Cluster your list into three to five core or compound values; for instance, my core value of Growth includes Courage, Learning and Creativity. Put your list of core values where you can see them every day, for instance on your desk or a screensaver. You can also anchor them with an object or picture that reminds you of them.

5 Consciously tune up living your values by choosing one and honouring it for a day. For instance, for Appreciation, you could start a meeting by offering it to people. With practice, consciously living your values will become second nature.

YOUR PURPOSE

What is the point of self-reflection and self-knowledge for leaders? If it is only for ourselves, we risk self-obsession, but when we return to the world through connecting with our higher purpose, we can be of service to it.

I F VALUES ARE THE COMPASS for your authentic leadership path, then purpose is your North Star. Teacher and author Parker J. Parker tells a story of how, during long winters in Minnesota, farmers would tie a rope from the back door of their houses to the door of their barns, to which they held to prevent becoming lost. This rope is like your purpose. In the blizzard of leadership demands, you can easily lose your way, your sense of who you are and *why* you are doing what you are doing. Never let go of your rope. The philosopher Friedrich Nietzsche wrote that 'he who has a *why* to live for, can bear almost any *how*.' Knowing why you want to lead gives you a deep well of energy to draw upon when things go well – and when they don't. Purpose is something bigger than you that works through you, but you can smooth its passage by being conscious and aligned with it.

We can clarify our values by listening to our lives. As a coach, I find the most useless questions are 'What is your purpose?' and 'What do you want?' They are too vague and overwhelming, and it is tempting to tackle them as you would an intellectual puzzle, when brainpower won't get you very far. Our sense of purpose comes from a deeper place within us, and to reach it, we need to use different approaches. I include in this chapter two approaches I use with clients: shifting perspective and visualization.

Shifting Perspective

The quality of our leadership and our lives depends less upon the answers we have, and more upon the kinds of questions we ask. For instance, we have a tendency to see ourselves as vehicles for the purpose of our organization or projects, but we can shift perspective by asking, 'Why have I hired or created my organization, business, project, relationship or life? How is it going to help me live my life's purpose?'

You can also tease out purpose by bringing to mind something you do every day, then climb the ladder towards purpose by asking, 'Why is that good?' Don't stop at one round. Whatever your response, follow each answer with, '…and why is that good?'. I suggest at least four rounds. Then you will start to enter the realm of higher purpose.

When we create a higher purpose ladder, it gives meaning to the most mundane or gruelling of tasks. In a folktale, three stonemasons in the Middle Ages were hard at work, when a visitor asked them what they were doing. The first stonemason snapped, 'I am cutting this stone.' The second stonemason, though less stressed, sighed, 'I'm building a parapet.' The

third stonemason beamed, 'I am building a beautiful cathedral in which countless people will worship God for centuries.' Here is someone with a sense of purpose.

Contemplation of Death

We can also clarify purpose by shifting our perspective to the end of our lives. As humans, we are born into a particular set of circumstances, which generate anxiety and require compassion: we know we are going to die, we don't want it to happen, and we don't know when it's going to happen. When we contemplate our death, we can reduce our fear of it. How do you want to feel at the end of your life? How will you know you lived your life fully? At the end of your life, you won't say 'I am so glad I emptied my inbox'. You will likely want to have lived an authentic life, to have fulfilled your potential, to have maintained meaningful relationships, to have spoken your truth, to have been kinder to yourself and others, and to have given yourself permission to be happier.

Contemplation of death can bring up resistance and fear. If you feel uncomfortable, let yourself soften. Credit your courage, rather than curse your anxiety. Thoughtful leadership is most essentially a search for meaning in full knowledge of the preciousness of our lives, and this is why it is a human and noble enterprise. As Apple founder Steve Jobs said at a famous commencement speech he gave in 2005, 'Remembering that you are going to die is the best way I know to avoid the

trap of thinking you have something to lose. You are already naked. There is no reason not to follow your heart.' He died six years later.

MINDFULNESS EXERCISE

THE DIFFERENCE YOU MADE

Visualization is a well-researched and effective method to bypass the conscious mind, which will analyze and focus on obstacles, and connect with the unconscious, which holds deeper desires and wishes. As always, take some time for yourself to do this exercise without interruption.

1 Close your eyes and take a few deep breaths.

2 Visualize yourself towards the end of your life as an old person. You are in a place where you feel comfortable and calm, perhaps in a garden or a favourite armchair. What do you see, hear, taste, touch and smell? Let gratitude fill you.

3 Imagine that in this place, people have gathered to honour you and your life. Either one-by-one, or in groups, they come to you and thank you for the difference you made in their lives and in the world. What are they thanking you for? Try not to overthink this. Note down what comes up as it will give you some pointers towards your life's purpose.

4 Based on this, begin to craft a declaration of purpose in any way that makes sense for you. It may take some time, so don't judge yourself if it doesn't spring forth at once. Anchor this with an image, object or piece of music, or by writing down your purpose state-ment, and keeping it where you can see it.

YOUR VISION

———————◆———————

As a leader, knowing your purpose is the first step on the path to putting it into action so that the world may benefit. The next step is to create and communicate a vision to give you and others a sense of direction and inspiration, grounded in reality, and energized by what is possible.

I HAVE A CARD ON MY DESK with an image of Green Tara, the Buddhist *bodhisattva* (an ideal of one who seeks Enlightenment) of compassionate action, sitting with one foot stepping forward. She reminds me to put my values into positive action in the world. What do you imagine is possible if you put your purpose into action? This is your vision. What we can imagine creates the reality of our world. Visioning asks us to imagine what doesn't exist today. It offers an image of where we are headed, inspires us to keep going through obstacles, focuses us and gives meaning to what we do. Ask yourself this series of questions, and write your answers down:

- What do you long for – in/for your life?
- What do you long for – for your loved ones?
- What do you long for – for your project, team, organization, business, gathering or community?
- What do you long for – for your country?
- What do you long for – for the world?

When we create a vision, we lead ourselves. When we

communicate it, we lead others. Leaders inspire themselves and others not through technical language, but through their use of images, symbolic language, metaphors and analogies to connect emotionally. In one of the most famous speeches of the twentieth century, 'I Have A Dream', Martin Luther King used metaphor, imagery and contrast: 'A state sweltering with the heat of injustice, sweltering with the heat of oppression, will be transformed into an oasis of freedom and justice.' Subsequent generations are still inspired by his vision.

Strategy without purpose and vision is an empty vessel. Leadership is dynamic. It has a direction and a process: purpose leads to vision, which then leads to strategy. Purpose is 'why', vision 'what' and strategy 'how'. Once you connect with purpose, you can start to create a vision of what this will look like in action, and develop your strategy to deliver it. Without purpose, your vision will not motivate you or inspire others, and your strategy will lack meaning and focus.

Questions Revisited

We live in a world our questions create – questions that help us see deeper, higher and further. Refer back to the questions I asked at the beginning of this chapter, on page 18.

What are you discovering? In this opening chapter, you have consciously connected with your authentic values and sense of purpose to use as compass and North Star on your path of thoughtful leadership. In the next chapter, we'll continue to hone this compass to notice your inner state at any moment and consciously choose how we want to be and what we want to do to realize our purpose and vision.

MINDFULNESS EXERCISE

FUTURE VISION

The technique of visualizing success as if it's already happened is used by elite sportspeople as well as leaders as part of their preparation, and the evidence backs this practice up. Take some time away from your everyday routine to do this exercise, and take notes after doing it.

1 Visualize yourself at a point in the future when you have achieved something that matters to you.

- What are you standing on?
- What are you wearing on the rest of your body?
- Where are you?
- What are the objects around you? Pay attention to their design and function.
- Imagine someone is coming towards you. Why are they coming to you? • What are you doing together? What are you saying to them and they to you?
- What difference are you making?
- How do you feel?

2 Create or find something to remind you of your vision, for instance a picture, mood board, piece of music, gesture or object.

3 Ask this future self for advice. If you are going to make this vision real, what's your first step?

CHAPTER TWO

LEADING YOURSELF

Self-awareness is your primary leadership skill.
You lead from yourself, with yourself. When the lens of
self-awareness is clouded, you suffer unnecessarily, and
others will too. Yet, there are gateways through which
we can return home to ourselves, and to our connection
with humanity, from where we can lead with wholeness.
To do this, we need to switch off automatic pilot and
develop self-leadership.

YOUR INNER STATE

In Western culture, we tend to regard our bodies as little more than brain-taxis. However, the body and mind are not separate entities. A thoughtful leader tunes into their whole self or body-mind, notices their inner state, and can consciously change it, leading themself for the benefit of themself, others and the world.

I MAGINE TWO RIVERS. One is the river of reality (or present awareness), and the other, the river of illusion (swirling with stories that our minds project onto ourselves, other people and the world). With practice, we can notice in which river we are immersed at any moment. Although swimming in the river of illusion is a very human tendency, it does have its dangers, which are amplified in leadership because of its wider and deeper impact. Thoughtful leaders bring exquisite self-awareness to the practice of leadership, and this is our subject for this chapter and the next. You'll practise and integrate three steps: *awareness*, *acceptance* and *choice*. Without awareness of our inner states and patterns, and the ability to choose self-leadership, we can react automatically, be carried away in the river of illusion, and so our impact is unconscious, and our ability to choose restricted. Without acceptance, we deny reality, or treat ourselves and others without compassion. Without awareness and acceptance, we don't have conscious choice how to respond.

The Self-Leadership Zone

We lead others thoughtfully when we can consciously lead ourselves. At any point on any day, we are either in the self-leadership zone or outside it. Outside the zone, we are on automatic, closed, defensive, committed to being right, and – if this becomes a default – we risk negative impact on ourselves, others and our projects. Inside the zone, we are open, curious, committed to learning, aware, emotionally intelligent, resilient and we feel positively motivated. If we apply discernment, rather than harsh judgment, we might notice when we are operating from love and positivity, with an interoceptive sensation of expansion, or from fear and negativity, experienced with contraction.

Take a moment now to check in on yourself. Are you inside or outside? In this chapter, we'll explore how to use interoception to tune into the sensations of the body, and mindfulness to objectively witness thoughts. My invitation for the next step on your leadership path is to integrate practices into your life that help you to lead from inside the zone.

The Unvirtuous Circle of Stress

Most people would like to avoid stress in their lives; leaders volunteer for more. In fact, they often thrive in stressful situations. Stress isn't bad in itself, but because of leaders' ongoing exposure, it can easily tip over the line to become default, toxic and counterproductive. Because stress is normal for leaders, and even addictive, we can be blind to our own stress reactions and patterns, and their effects on others.

People are acutely sensitive to the emotional states of their leaders, and often create stories based on their perceptions:

A Coaching Story: An Unthoughtful Leader

A client was a marketing director in a national campaigning organization. When I met her, she was ready to hand in her resignation, and she was not alone. Over 70 percent of the leadership team had quit in the previous year, and as a result, long-term planning was non-existent, and day-to-day operations chaotic. This anecdote goes some way to explaining why. The directors and their reports were in a workshop on communication skills. The CEO arrived late and highly agitated. She had just come from a meeting that had angered her and, rather than noticing her state, and taking steps to calm herself, she proceeded to disrupt the session by throwing herself noisily into a chair, launching barbed comments that undermined the facilitator and participants. A more self-aware leader would notice her toxic stress level, and apply ways to self-regulate to prevent negative impact. This incident explains the campaign's difficulties in retaining talent, motivating staff and reducing the amount of time off taken by staff for stress-related health issues.

---

they might assume that you think negatively of them, that you don't have their interests at heart, or that, if they tell you bad news, they will be blamed. Those stories calcify into beliefs that affect their behaviour towards you. So, of course, you trust them less, which creates an unvirtuous circle. Stress is contagious and spreads like a virus leaving everyone – including patient zero – exhausted, miserable and burnt out. It takes us across the line, outside the self-leadership zone, and into the river of illusion. Let's walk that line by understanding more about what stress is and how it manifests.

The Neurophysiology of Stress

About 50,000 years ago, two clans sat around on the plains of Africa. They noticed an unfamiliar creature coming towards them, and while one clan lingered to watch the sun glinting off its teeth, the other leapt into action, grabbed their young and ran away. Not surprisingly, we are the descendants of the second clan. So finely tuned are we to threat, that our survival stress reactions are triggered not only by real and present danger, but by imagined or perceived threat, uncertainty and the unknown. Our problem today is that an email triggers those same stress reactions as a long-ago predator. Stress is normal and welcome in some respects, but we need to master it as consciously as possible to lead ourselves and others well. To do that, we need to start by undoing the notion that 'body' and 'mind' are separate.

The Five Stress Patterns

All forms of stress reaction are short-term survival strategies. Once triggered by a real or imagined stimulus, our automatic stress reactions have five potential expressive forms: *fight*, *flight* and the less-known *freeze, fold* and *friend* (or *fawn*). Some psychologists suggest that the freeze, fold and friend patterns habituate in childhood, when a child may not be able to fight or flee a stressful situation at home, for instance. A stressful situation for an adult may re-trigger childhood trauma. In the following list, notice which patterns seem familiar to you; there may be more than one.

● **Fight:** confrontation, sometimes aggression, self-righteousness and/or argument.

● **Flight**: escape, avoidance and withdrawal of emotional connection, such as looking at your phone, cracking a joke or changing the subject.

● **Freeze**: locked-in, unable to express, overwhelmed.

● **Fold**: collapse, giving up, victimhood and sense of absence of agency, with thoughts such as, 'This always happens to me'.

● **Friend** or **fawn**: often a secondary stress reaction, trying to smooth things over and 'be friends'. This is a reactive pattern to stress and a need to relieve it, not to be confused with the healthier practice of keeping emotional connection while maintaining boundaries, even in conflict.

The 'body-mind' is intimately connected and integrated. The body is not a brain-taxi, carrying our executive functions to and from meetings. We are not 'in' our bodies; we *are* our bodies. Our embodied inner state has a profound effect on others. The state of our bodies affects the state of our minds, and a thought will affect our bodies. In workshops, I sometimes playfully state that I can change the physiology of people in the room in an instant, a claim usually greeted with skepticism. Suddenly I yell 'Bang!', and most people automatically jump. What's happening in that moment?

Something happens or a thought pops up in your head. Almost instantly, the sympathetic branch of your autonomic nervous system activates, directing the body's rapid involuntary reaction to dangerous or stressful situations. The sympathetic nervous system functions like an accelerator in a car. It provides the body with energy so that it can survive danger. The parasympathetic nervous system acts like a brake, which slows down and soothes body-mind after the danger has passed.

Even on a day without a major stress event, we will be reacting to countless small stressors: the phone rings, an email notification pops up, a colleague interrupts us, someone pushes in front of us on the train platform, our partners or children want attention when we are tired, a deadline is imminent, or we see something we value but can't have. If external stimuli were not enough, thoughts and impulses

run like triggering tickertape throughout our day, until we lie in bed at night worrying about the next day's presentation, that our loved one hasn't called, or about the meaning of life.

Useful & Toxic Stress

Stress isn't a reflection of your leadership ability. There is nothing wrong with stress; it's natural and normal. In our modern, technologically driven lives, it's easy to forget that we are animals with smart phones, trying to live in complex social groupings. We tend to use the word 'stress' as a cover-all for discomfort, unhappiness and unwelcome agitation. But I like to make a distinction between 'useful stress', for instance, feeling excited and motivated, and 'toxic stress', which demotivates or has other negative effects. I also want to make clear that we wouldn't want to live in a world of universal serenity. Without agitation, people wouldn't have fought for civil and human rights, for instance. We need a healthy amount of useful stress to keep what psychologists term a 'growing edge', and to change what needs changing.

However, there's a point at which stress can become our default go-to, with the result that we react rather than respond to situations. Over time, this deeply affects our mental, physical, emotional and spiritual health. The brain becomes less successful at focusing, problem-solving, emotional control and empathy. We reduce our capability to see the big picture, to be creative and innovative, to be kind to others as well as

---

Early Toxic Stress Signals

• Sunday Night Syndrome: dreading going to work on Monday.

• Over-reactions to small stuff, such as losing a parking space, or a computer running slow.

• Heightened sensitivity to noise and light.

• Irritability and snappiness.

• Feeling overwhelmed daily.

• Sleep disturbance.

• Aches and pains, especially in the back, neck and head.

• Increased 'comfort' behaviour, such as unhealthy eating or drinking alcohol.

• Indigestion and heartburn.

• Difficulty switching off.

• Lower immune system and feeling rundown.

• Negative thoughts and self-talk.

• The desire to walk away from it all.

---

ourselves, to feel excited and joyful, to collaborate, and to make the impact we want. We burnout at huge cost to our lives, families, communities, societies and economies.

Whether you are an industrialist or an activist, as a leader in a world that is volatile, uncertain, complex and ambiguous, the stress switch can become jammed on, with inevitable negative consequences. Chronic exhaustion, depression and anxiety, high blood pressure, immune suppression, gastrointestinal issues, back pain and heart problems, insomnia, substance abuse and alcoholism, and relationship and family breakdown are aspects of leadership we seldomly discuss in public, but which are constant dangers. The difference between healthy stress and burnout is a matter of degree, which means the earlier you recognize some of these signs, the better. Poker players say we all have unique 'tells' or signs that we are under stress. One of my tells manifests in tension in the muscles of my pelvis, for instance, and I check in and gently unclench this part of my body throughout my day. Some clients notice tension in their shoulders. When you practise mindful awareness, you'll notice your tells. So, let's start building some skilfulness in noticing our inner state.

AWARENESS

Even in the centre of what can feel like a storm, leaders need to be able to tune in to themselves, to others and to the situation. To do this requires skilfulness in cultivating present awareness — or, quite simply, switching off automatic, and noticing.

SIT STILL FOR TEN MINUTES, and every time you have a thought, make a mark on a piece of paper. It never ceases to amaze me how quickly we can fill a page. Our minds

generate tens of thousands of thoughts a day, leaping from one to another in rapid cascades, causing stress reactions throughout our bodies, even on a micro-level. It's as if the mind runs ahead and we chase it, overwhelmed. But we are not our thoughts. We are people having thoughts.

The one who witnesses thoughts, without being led by them, is the deeper, wiser self. In practising mindful awareness, we develop our sense of this deeper self, and are less at the whim of what meditation and mindfulness teachers call our 'monkey minds'. We want to lead from here, but it can be challenging for leaders for several reasons.

Leaders live in their heads a lot of the time, and are bombarded by other people's thoughts and desires all day. As they grasp for the future, leaders can be impatient with the present. If you feel a resistance to or discomfort with stillness, it may be that you fear slowing down, as if your thoughts are butterflies that need to be trapped and nailed down in case you lose them forever. I am not saying this is wrong. But we connect with ourselves and others in the present: it is here we start all our endeavours, and know what is available. The work of developing mindful awareness is challenging. The mind will head off like a curious child again and again. It is the nature of the mind to do so. But think of driving a car. Would you let a small child drive? Through practising awareness, you can notice the child in the driver's seat, move it into the passenger seat and put your wise adult self behind the wheel.

MINDFULNESS EXERCISE

BODY SCAN TO NOTICE YOUR INNER STATE

Practise this several times a day, whether you consciously feel stressed or not, to develop greater self-awareness, and rewire your nervous system from a stressed default. You can sit, lie or stand.

1 Take a couple of breaths. If thoughts come to mind, notice them without following them, and bring your attention back to your breath, as you would gently but firmly call back a small child who has wandered off.

2 Slowly scan your body upwards from your feet towards your head, gently noticing any sensations without labelling or judgment, for instance, weight, pressure, temperature and contact with surfaces. If you don't feel anything, accept it exactly as it is. There's no right or wrong, and no goal.

3 Have a sense of your whole body here right now, as it is. If you notice discomfort or pain, don't focus on it; let it be one sensation in a field of sensations, which is your body in this moment. If you feel sharp pain, move to be more comfortable.

4 Hold your attention on your body for a minute or two, and notice if anything changes.

5 Bring to mind one word that describes how you feel right now. Pay attention to sensations, rather than your interpretation of them: 'tight' rather than 'anxious', for instance. The point here is not to reach a zen-like level of calm, but to notice what is happening right now.

Embodiment

What are you aware of in your body right now? Our culture encourages us to be profoundly disembodied, with hours spent in front of screens doing cognitive and intellectual labour. The practice of awareness, without stories about what's going on, or judgments about what should or shouldn't be happening, anchors us in the river of reality. Leaders need to develop and practise interoceptive self-awareness to check stress and unconscious behaviour, and this starts by noticing our embodied inner state. When we do so, self-awareness becomes our default: we can track our inner state while paying attention to what we are doing simultaneously. Our whole embodied selves are a rich source of information for us as leaders, and when we develop deeper awareness, our leadership and our lives are enriched. Compared with living only from our heads, it's like returning home.

Aversion & Grasping

Falling in love, panicking, learning or being hungry, like all inner states, involve a series of neurochemical, physical and mental processes. We label these sensations 'good' (for example, excitement) or 'bad' (anxiety), depending on whether or not we want them, or have a sense of control over them. Think of 'wanting' or 'not wanting' as wrappers around sensations, thoughts and experiences. These wrappers are the source of our suffering. Buddhists call them 'aversion' (not

Here I Am

I sometimes meditate with a group. Once, after we had meditated for thirty minutes, our teacher invited questions. A woman said, 'I feel so calm and centered. But I know that when I open the door and see the bus, all my calm will vanish in an instant. How do I stay in this bubble?'

'Meditation is not about creating a bubble of calmness,' the teacher replied. 'It is simply to notice, witness and accept wherever you are at that moment. So, "Here I am, feeling rushed. Here I am, running for the bus."'

You will get triggered, and your mind will wander off. Keep returning to present-awareness with the simple reminder: 'Here I Am.' Incorporate this practice into your life, and your self-awareness and self-acceptance will flourish.

wanting) or 'grasping' (wanting very much). We feel aversion to pain and loneliness, and grasp for happiness and those experiences we believe will generate it. If someone offers you a great deal of money or the promise of sex, grasping or 'pleasure stress' has the same effect on your body-mind as aversion stress, such as a racing heart and narrowed focus.

Leaders make many decisions based on grasping and aversion. A thoughtful leader discerns the effect these states have on them and can mitigate them to see things clearly. Later in

the chapter, when we explore the topic of 'choice', we'll explore how being in a state of aversion or grasping uncentres us, and how to re-centre ourselves.

With practice, you'll notice that, rather than being fixed, we are in a constant process of change, which you can influence. By integrating practices of awareness into your everyday life, such as doing regular check-ins on your inner state before you walk into a meeting, make a call or have a difficult conversation, you'll be able to be more present. With regular integrated practice, techniques such as centring, body scanning and meditation can help us rewire our brains and nervous systems from default stress and aversion and grasping, to greater equanimity.

ACCEPTANCE

Once we are aware, we need to practise acceptance, rather than resistance —acceptance of reality over the stories we tell ourselves about ourselves and the world, and acceptance of ourselves and others with compassion.

I ONCE LED A LEADERSHIP WORKSHOP with a group of senior healthcare managers. When I introduced the practice of acceptance and compassion, they bristled. 'Isn't that about being *soft?*' The word swilled around the room like an unpleasant taste in the mouth, as if heresy to the doctrine of effective

leadership. This resistance derives its energy from a misunderstanding of what acceptance and compassion are, and from the protective shield around some fears that leaders have.

Acceptance and compassion don't prevent us from having boundaries, or holding ourselves and others responsible. Acceptance means acknowledging the reality of a situation, and not resisting what you cannot or choose not to change. It doesn't mean you agree or approve of it. Compassion is seeing the humanity in us all, believing we are all doing our best at any time, and wanting to address the causes of suffering. In the process of awareness, acceptance and choice, acceptance is vital, for without the ability to see things as they are and feel our shared humanity, we become armoured, hardened and disconnected from ourselves and from people, the same people we want to inspire, engage and serve.

Why Compassion is Hard

Far from being a 'soft' skill, practising compassion is hard for several reasons. First, we are trying to re-train our automatic reactions and form new habits, which is hard for all of us, and requires humility – an essential, though sometimes challenging, leadership quality. Second, most leaders are developed or chosen to lead with their heads, not their hearts. Third, we can feel that we need to check our emotions at the door when we become leaders, as we take on more responsibility and pressure, and so can be less tolerant of vulnerability.

Fourth, compassion can be seen as a weakness, rather than a strength – something that gets in the way of achieving 'hard' outcomes, or worse, something that will leave us exposed to be exploited. Fifth, all leaders have a powerful inner driver, which keeps pushing them onwards and upwards, demanding more of themselves and others. Most leaders with whom I have worked have difficulty discerning the point at which this driver has stopped being useful and started being toxic.

Many a leader has confessed to me they fear losing their edge if they practise acceptance and compassion. But this is to misunderstand and underestimate the value of these practices. The best leaders have both spine and heart: courage to make tough decisions, and compassion to connect with the human impact. Graduates at US military academy West Point cite 'connection and care' as the key qualities that defines a good leader. On the battlefield, knowing their commander cares about them makes it easier to trust and follow them.

Neuroimaging studies show that practising compassion regulates the functioning of the limbic system, the site in the brain responsible for processing emotions and empathy. Research suggests compassionate leaders produce better results because they connect emotionally, inspire loyalty, don't avoid difficult decisions and conversations, and have greater ability to look long-term. Toning up benevolent emotions reduces negative thinking, broadens our perspective, increases creativity and resilience, and breaks down barriers

we erect between ourselves and others. We can choose to make that switch in a moment, and through regular practice we can begin to feel its effects on our leadership, as the brain rewires from reactiveness to responsiveness and connection.

Self-Compassion

The first step to practising acceptance and compassion is often the most challenging, but the most essential. After their initial resistance, the cohort of senior healthcare managers at the workshop wrote themselves a letter from the perspective of a compassionate friend – an exercise I include in the box opposite. They were astonished by their experience. As they wrote, they became aware of how hard they were being on themselves, the stress and anguish it caused them, and how practising self-compassion released capabilities and resources to support themselves, and the people around them.

A compassionate leader sees and accepts all of themselves. They know their vulnerabilities and can accept themselves, not to justify unreasonable behaviour, but because they know that no one is perfect, and don't want to cause additional suffering to themselves and others. Perfectionism is like a weak dose of insanity: an open invitation for anxiety and obsessive thinking, and an obstacle to completing projects and keeping good relationships with people around you. Self-compassion asks that we take responsibility for ourselves. Once we can offer that to ourselves, we can model it to others.

MINDFULNESS EXERCISE

THE SELF-COMPASSION LETTER

Practise this exercise especially when you notice you are being hard on yourself.

1 Close your eyes. Bring to mind someone (real or imaginary) who is unconditionally loving, accepting, kind and compassionate. Imagine that this person can see all your strengths and all your weaknesses.

2 Write a letter to yourself from the perspective of this person. What would they say to you? How would they convey the compassion they feel for you, especially for the pain you feel when you judge yourself so harshly? What would they say to remind you that you are human? If you feel stuck, start with, 'I know all your imperfections and vulnerabilities, and I accept them and know that you are doing the best you can.'

Compassion for Others

We sometimes support others before ourselves, but self-compassion is a must-have for leaders. In leadership, when we drop self-compassion, we increase the chances of burnout, and are less tolerant of others, uncertainty and uncomfortable feelings. Once you have toned up your ability to feel compassion for yourself, then you can extend this to others.

I recommend you try the practice of loving-kindness or *metta bhavana* and track the effects on your leadership. One of my clients found it beneficial, as she had developed the habit

of helping her team by taking on their work. This is not compassion, it is breaking your own boundaries, and training people into learned helplessness. It felt like an easy fix in the short-term, but in the long-term it elevated her stress, and was no real support to her junior colleagues. After integrating compassion practice into her life, she understood their struggle without feeling irritated, and set aside time to coach them, developing their potential. Her team flourished and her stress – and unnecessary workload – decreased. So much for a 'soft' skill.

Our Shared Humanity

Acceptance and compassion are not demonstrated by buying doughnuts for the team, fixing situations and people, or avoiding hard decisions and difficult conversations. It's not about faking that you care. Compassion brings us closer to each other, rather than reinforcing our separateness.

Our human compassion binds us the one to
the other – not in pity or patronizingly, but as human
beings who have learnt how to turn our common
suffering into hope for the future.

Nelson Mandela (1918–2013)
ANTI-APARTHEID REVOLUTIONARY, POLITICAL LEADER AND PHILANTHROPIST,
WHO SERVED AS PRESIDENT OF SOUTH AFRICA FROM 1994 TO 1999

We recognize and tolerate our individual and shared suffering, rather than ignoring, avoiding or fearing it. Compassionate practices help us work together towards a common good by connecting us with the fundamental situation of our humanity: that we suffer. We know we are going to die, and we suffer. We fear loss and pain, and we suffer. German Chancellor Angela Merkel demonstrated this in a speech in 2020 during the coronavirus crisis:

'This is what an epidemic shows us: how vulnerable we all are, how dependent we are on the considerate behaviour of others, but also how we can protect and strengthen each other by acting together. It depends on everyone.'

Compassion connects us to each other, no matter what our circumstances.

CHOICE

Once we come off automatic pilot, notice our inner state, and can accept it with compassion, then we can ask ourselves, 'How do I want to be in this moment? What do I choose? What impact do I want to have? What would be most useful right now?'

W E HAVE MORE CONSCIOUS CHOICE over our inner state than we realize. But this doesn't mean we don't get triggered. At the end of every class, Morihei Ueshiba, the founder of the martial art of aikido, would step into the centre of the dojo, and invite all his students to challenge him at once. His students marvelled, 'Master, how is it that you are never triggered by whatever comes at you?' 'Oh no,' the master replied, 'I get triggered all the time. But I regain my composure so quickly, you don't even notice.' If a master like Ueshiba experienced natural triggers, then it is unrealistic for us to aim for a plateau of consistent calm. Leaders experience random incoming demands and challenges all day, and feeling triggered is normal and understandable. We need to notice our state, accept it and then choose to regain composure and a sense of mastery over ourselves.

Centring

We cannot always choose what happens in our lives, but we can choose how to respond to it. Aikido offers a useful tool to regain self-mastery. When triggered, Ueshiba was able to compose himself in an instant by centring. As the body and mind are not separate, we can work through the body to affect the mind. Centring techniques change us physically, neuro-logically, cognitively and emotionally. It's not a short cut to zen calm, but dials down unhelpful automatic reactivity.

Leaders need to integrate regular centring practices into their lives. I ask my clients to imagine the benefits of feeling ten percent calmer. This will do more for you than a fortnight on a beach. Stress isn't an illness. It doesn't go away when you take a break or medicate yourself. Practising centring daily,

MINDFULNESS EXERCISE

SIX DIRECTIONS BREATH

✳

This is a lovely slow form of centring practice, which can also be a diagnostic for awareness of what you might need.

1 Sit quietly with your eyes shut. Breathe in.

2 As you exhale, visualize that you are pushing your breath downwards. Perhaps you have a sense of your breath going through the floor to the centre of the earth. There is no right or wrong, notice how it feels to you.

3 Breathe in again, then as you exhale, visualize pushing your breath into the space above you and notice how that feels.

4 Breathe in again, and visualize pushing your breath out your left side; on your next out-breath, visualize doing the same out your right side.

5 Inhale, and with your next exhale, imagine that you are pushing your breath out into the space behind you, as if your back opens to let it out. Repeat for the space in front.

6 Finally, take a few breaths imagining you are exhaling in all six directions at once. Notice how you feel.

7 To add a diagnostic layer, notice how you feel in each direction and if you sense any weakness or blockage. This might offer a suggestion for what you need. Here are some things/questions to ask yourself:

- Down – 'How grounded do I feel?'
- Up – 'How inspired, creative and/or confident do I feel?'
- Left – 'Am I listening, receiving and being?'
- Right – 'Am I taking action?'
- Left and right – 'Am I including and connecting with others?'
- Behind – 'Who and what has my back?' These can be people, those who came before you, and/or your own story.
- Front – 'Am I behaving with integrity? Is my inner self in alignment with how I am acting and with what I am doing?'

These enquiries aren't fixed, so with practice you may create your own resonant/personalized questions.

several times a day, will rewire your stress reactions more effectively. The trick is remembering to do it. However, with regular practice, it becomes habit.

Centring works by releasing key points in your body that tense when triggered. When stressed, we narrow our attention to the point of threat and can miss what else is available in the big picture; centring unwinds this through cultivating an expansive perspective. We have trained ourselves to pull in our awareness, and this is the opposite of what we need to develop as leaders. Expanded awareness of self and others increases leadership presence.

YOUR INNER CRITIC & INNER ALLY

Who is leading you from within? Can you tune into the voice of wisdom, clarity, compassion and courage through which thoughtful leadership speaks? How much is your leadership impacted by the voices of judgment, self-doubt and comparison? How can you choose to lead from your deeper, wiser self?

IN A FOLKTALE ATTRIBUTED TO THE CHEROKEE PEOPLE, two wolves hang around the edges of a camp. One is a vicious beast who would rip out your throat and kill your babies. The other is a proud creature who will protect the camp if you reach agreement. In a fight, which one would win? The answer is, the one you feed.

Energy follows attention. We all have Inner Critics: that inner voice of judgment that say you're not enough – not smart enough, experienced enough, attractive enough, loveable enough or rich enough, for example. But when we feed it, let it take the wheel of our lives, treat it as if it is the voice of truth and reality, rather than the voice of perception, then we forfeit self-mastery, and it will rip us apart and sabotage new ideas, relationships and potential. As a result, we don't step forward and up as leaders, we keep ourselves and our ambitions small. We stay in our comfort zones. We overcompensate, hoping no one will notice how insecure we feel. It's as if we have our Inner Critics on speed dial. Under stress and out of habit, we seem to have lost our connection with our Inner Ally, that wiser self who encourages and supports us if nourished.

Whether you feed Critic or Ally is your choice. To lead yourself and others consciously, you'll need to notice when the Inner Critic is in the driver's seat, accept it rather than doubling down on yourself for having it, and choose to make your Inner Ally your co-pilot.

The Origins of the Inner Critic

Inner Critics are psychological constructs we develop in childhood to protect ourselves from shame and rejection from the relationships we rely upon for physical and psychological safety. From birth and throughout childhood, we are so vulnerable we need the protection of others for survival. As a result, we are acutely sensitive to perceived threats of rejection. Our psychological scouts morph into our Inner Critics. The child internalizes what they believe are indicators of such threats – such as a parent getting cross at disruptive behaviour, or a playground group calling out some random infringement – then renders the perceived messages general, pervasive and very loud, without the emotional maturity to keep perspective.

When, as adults, we face situations that are novel and uncertain, or that trigger our fears of rejection, failure or vulnerability, our Inner Critics try to keep us safe by warning us to stay in our comfort zone. To get our attention they don't enquire, 'Have you prepared enough?', in a nuanced, adult way; instead, they panic, 'You'll fail and look like a fool.' Inner Critics are the vestiges of a Childhood Survival Strategy programme, which is still running in us as adults, like an old operating system. Think of them as loyal soldiers, fighting a war that has ended. No one has told them that the war is over, that feeling psychologically vulnerable is no longer a warning of danger to survival.

I hope you take some comfort from understanding that the Inner Critic is normal. But this doesn't mean we can allow our negative self-talk to run our lives and leadership, which it can do unless we take responsibility for it. We're running an old programme. It's time for an upgrade.

Inner Critics

Let me introduce you to the family of Inner Critics and their typical scripts. There is more than one and you may be able to add your own:

- The Judge: you're never good enough.
- The Pleaser: to be accepted you need to make others happy.
- The Rule Maker: if you meet or fall short of certain criteria, you won't be enough.
- The Perfectionist: to be valued you must be perfect.
- The Comparer: everyone else is better than you.
- The Doubter: you can't do this.
- The Stern Parent: you're such a loser for not getting this.
- The Indulgent Parent: it's not fair you have to do it, so do something easier instead.

I have worked with many different kinds of leaders from different fields, and the inner voices are the same. Yet so many people lean back from leadership, imagining that leaders are a blessed breed apart, mercifully free of Inner Critics. Not in my experience. All leaders are human and vulnerable.

If you don't take responsibility for your Inner Critic tendencies and patterns, they will unconsciously run you. When you notice your Inner Critic by spotting the familiar script or physical tension, practise centring. Name it, to separate it from your deeper, wiser self, using the titles above or your own characterization. For instance, I have an Inner Auditor,

who turns up when I am trying to be creative, with a hundred reasons why my delicate new idea could never be a revenue spinner. I thank him, and ask him to come back when I need his forensic appraisal to file my taxes.

Sometimes, the voice of our Inner Critic is trying to convey something useful, such as our need to prepare. Sometimes what frightens it is not fear of failure, but fear of success. We are all wary of the unknown. Uncertainty doesn't sit well with us. Leaders thoughtfully temper Inner Critics so as to live more comfortably on that growing edge, where leaders need to be, with the unknown and uncertain as companions. Great leaders, having managed their own Inner Critics, make it more comfortable for others to do the same. Stay humble: Inner Critics will get into the driving seat at times, but as soon as you notice, don't beat yourself up. Move them away and shift your wiser, adult self into its place instead.

Inner Allies

In the folktale, there are two wolves. The critic is only one of these. There is also the one who dares, who supports, and who believes in you – an Inner Ally. Each of us has Inner Allies: deep resources of wisdom, clarity, compassion and courage from which we can draw. Here are a few members of this family:

• The Appreciative One: who sees what is good about this moment.

- The Sage: who sees what's really going on under the surface.
- The Mountaineer: who, rather than being overwhelmed when they look up at the mountain, gathers what they need, and takes the first step.
- The Compassionate Friend: the one who supports you as you would support another.
- The Explorer: the one who embraces an opportunity for adventure.
- The Seer: who holds on to the longer-term perspective.
- The Good Parent: who acknowledges your fear, and won't abandon you as you try.
- The Storyteller: who reminds you of everything you have already overcome.

Imagine a table around which sit your own Inner Allies, ready and willing for you to call upon them. You are welcome to include people you know or public figures. When I feel prickles of insecurity about aging, I imagine what Helen Mirren would say, and the reply includes laughter, a confident tilt of the chin, and some juicy language.

We can also call upon our unconscious through visualization to give us the Inner Ally we need, an exercise I include on page 66. What would your Inner Allies say to you at this moment in your life? For instance, an agency founder and CEO with whom I worked gave a great deal to people around him, but not enough to himself. Within his Inner Ally

MINDFULNESS EXERCISE

YOUR INNER ALLY

Visualization doesn't work all the time with all people, so don't worry if you feel you are not getting it. It can be useful to record the instructions and then listen back to them.

1 Find a time and place where you won't be disturbed, and sit with your eyes closed, if that's comfortable for you.

2 Visualize yourself on a path or walking down a corridor. It can be a place you know or imagine. You might be in a building, or in nature. Pay attention to what you can see and hear. You feel at ease, calm and safe. In front of you is a door towards which you are walking. What do you notice about this door? Approach the door and stand in front of it. Beyond this door, your Inner Ally is waiting to meet you. How do you feel as you stand here?

3 Open the door and walk through. Notice the environment you're in.

4 You encounter your Ally in this place. This could be a living being, or a fantastical figure; it could be an object; it could also be immaterial, a glow of light, a sensation or a sound, for instance. Whatever comes up is fine; there is no right or wrong. If nothing comes, that's fine too. Allow yourself to receive your Ally with deep gratitude. This Ally knows everything about you, accepts you unconditionally, and has wisdom, clarity, compassion and courage. What do you notice about your Ally?

5 Ask your Ally these questions and listen for any response. If nothing comes, don't push, we're just 'shaking the tree'.

• What is important for me to know about you?

• What do you want for me?

• How might I access your wisdom, clarity, compassion and courage easily? Is there a name I can call you?

6 Now your Ally gives you something. Receive it. What is it? Ask your Ally, 'What is important for me to know about this?'

When you are ready, take your leave of your Ally, knowing you can consciously connect to the source of leadership within yourself.

visualization, he encountered his dog, friendly, faithful, always happy to see him, a source of unconditional love who encouraged him to take care of himself. Another client, a senior business manager, visualized a bright yellow diamond that helped him access his inner clarity. A community leader felt a point of light inside her chest fill her with power and gratitude. A green economy entrepreneur visualized her grandmother holding her hand, an image she returned to when she felt anxiety about her new project. A creative consultant saw an Amazonian warrior who gave her power and strength. A composer visualized a block of silver liquid like mercury in which he could immerse himself and re-emerge transformed. Our unconscious often speaks to us in images and body sensations, yet we often tune these out as 'noise'. A thoughtful leader stays open and curious to their unconscious for the rich information it sends every day.

We have stayed in the inner world from which thoughtful leadership emerges. Now let's stand on the bridge between ourselves and others, bringing with us awareness, acceptance and choice, to see where those choices might take us: what and how we might choose to be and do, to meet whatever is in front and ahead of us with adaptability, grace and integrity.

CHAPTER THREE

LEADING WITH SELF-AWARENESS & CHOICE

The essence of a leader's power is their impact. A thoughtful leader ensures that, as much as possible, this is conscious and positive. While remaining authentic, we need to consciously choose how to lead the many changing situations we face. In this chapter, we explore leadership energies to help develop awareness of our leadership range and choice. We also need to be courageously honest about our unconscious negative tendencies or 'shadow', less we cause more harm than good through our leadership.

LEADERSHIP ENERGIES

◆

Leadership is energy in motion, harnessed and directed. All of us have elemental energetic preferences, which are the signatures of our leadership style. As leaders, we need to be aware of the range of leadership energies available, and our habits and preferences within these, so we can take responsibility and employ our energies for the greater good.

WE SEE THE WORLD IN FIXED, material terms, but everything in it is energy, interacting and transforming. Your awareness of and skilfulness with your own energetic range and choices deeply impacts the people around you, your projects and the world. Thoughtful leaders consciously develop range to adapt to whatever the circumstances demand. Ironically, success can sabotage us. If we believe that one way of being or acting as a leader brings great results, we can wear down a groove repeating it, then blame ourselves and others when the magic doesn't work again. With energetic range, we can tune into what's needed in the moment, and bring a congruent, deliberate facet of leadership out into the world.

The four elemental energies of leadership are Fire, Earth, Air and Water. All four are vital elements we need to harness: to be decisive and directional (Fire), grounded and attentive (Earth), visionary and innovative (Air), and connected and

EXPLORING THE FOUR ELEMENTS

❋

Take some time to explore your relationship with each energy in the embodied experiments below.

1 Step decisively into Fire:

• Focus on an object or spot with purpose, and let your whole body be oriented in that direction. Say 'Yes' boldly. Now firmly thrust out your hand in front of you, palm turned up and front, and say, with comparable assertiveness, 'No'. Fire decides yes or no, and sets clear boundaries.

• Notice how that feels. Do you enjoy the feeling, or is it uncomfortable? Amplify and reduce it; slow it down until you feel comfortable.

2 Now line up for the element of Earth:

• Sit straight, feet symmetrical on the floor. Order yourself and objects around you. Earth cannot tolerate mess.

• What do you notice? Do you feel secure or restricted? How much order or mess can you tolerate before you start to feel an edge?

3 Next, spring into the element of Air:

• Sit on the edge of your chair, or if you can, jump up on your toes and move around quickly and lightly, arms above your head. Look up. Be spontaneous.

• Do you feel unnerved or free? Are you worried you look idiotic? How long can you keep it up? Air can be exhausting.

4 Finally, soften and flow into the element of Water:

• Openly move your hips and torso. Expand outwards, opening your arms and chest. If there is a noise, object or person close by, relate to it or them.

• Does this come naturally and comfortably to you? Or would you prefer to go back to another energy? If so, which?

5 For each energy, ask yourself: What would it feel like and look like to lead from this energy? Are there situations in my leadership where leading from this energy would be helpful? Can I recognize and appreciate this element in others, and meet people where they feel comfortable? Can I help them develop their strengths for the benefit of all?

collaborative (Water). None of the elemental energies has a pre-determined strength or intensity; fire can be a furnace, or a single flame. These are not fixed types, more preferred or habitual energies that you lead with.

We often have untrue and out-of-date stories about our-selves from which we operate as leaders. For instance, I always believed I led with Water, until I tested this theory by asking for feedback, and discovered that I also brought a lot of Fire and Air to my leadership. I was denying this because of my aversion to associations with aggression and danger. Psycho-logically, they were in my shadow, a concept we'll explore later in this chapter. You may have one or two elements towards which you feel discomfort. We can build awareness of our authentic energetic leadership elements through feed-back from others, but also from our direct interoceptive experience, our ability to feel and understand what we sense inside our bodies, such as aversion or grasping. There's no right or wrong, or good or bad. We're reaping the wisdom that our bodies hold to become more consciously aware.

Leadership Range

Without range across all of the essential leadership elements, we limit our situational choice (we'll develop this further soon). Where we know ourselves to be weak with a cost to our leadership impact, we need to take responsibility and develop these areas, or ensure we have people next to us who

support us with their strength in an area of our weakness. Excess in a leadership element can be equally dangerous. Once you notice, be self-compassionate and consciously commit to developing your leadership range across all elements, if possible.

Cultivate the elements by working through the body to tone the mind. If you lack Fire, engage in practices that develop it, for instance, combat martial arts help manage fear of conflict. You can develop Earth through precise practices such as tai chi. If you need to develop Air, improvisation helps you think in the moment and let go of the fear of looking foolish. Flow practices such as some dance, moving meditations or creative drawing can develop Water energy, as can responding to another in Contact Improvisation or aikido. You can also do something simple such as walking, but embody an energetic element in your way of doing it.

For excesses, develop your comfort with energy in another modifying element: Water and Earth bank Fire; Air and Fire free us from being stuck in the mud of Earth; Fire and Earth give Water clarity and direction; Earth grounds Air. When I have too much Air, I spring from idea to idea, without building bridges from one to the other. When I notice this, I practise walking with the quality of Earth to ground myself, ensuring my foot is planted on the ground before lifting the next, being slower and more deliberate. Determine your next step to develop range, then try it and track the results.

Energetic Weaknesses & Excesses

For leaders, energetic deficiencies or excesses are problematic. Ignore them at your peril; if you do they will come back to bite you.

Fire

Too little – Goals are unclear; decisions don't get made; boundaries are weak.

Too much – Dismissive of alternative views; danger of 'summit fever' where we focus too tightly on a goal.

Earth

Too little – 'Winging it'; impatience; lack of processes, policies, procedures and follow through.

Too much – Don't see big picture; avoid risks; resist new ideas; become entangled in processes, procedures and policies.

Air

Too little – Lack of creativity and innovation; no higher purpose or big picture, leading to demotivation.

Too much – No follow-through on ideas; impatient with details; risk losing connection with others.

Water

Too little – Go-it-alone attitude; lack of connection with others; inability to listen.

Too much – Lack of decision-making; no boundaries.

Situational Leadership Choice

In thoughtful leadership you make a conscious choice to lead from several possible dimensions, skilfully switching from one to another as the circumstances and the needs of the moment require. If you find it hard to switch easily, then start by building awareness of whatever mode you are in at any time of the day, and ask yourself, 'Is this useful right now?' Rather than fixing in one preferred element, use them situationally, switching and mixing elements together.

Leading from Fire

As a leader, you will face situations that require you to consciously choose the elemental energy of Fire. For instance, at the beginning of a project, you take a stand, give direction and define goals. As you go on, you sense when the time for talk is done and ideas need to be pinned down into action, and communicate this clearly.

We also need to switch out of Fire in certain situations lest it cause more harm than good. A client left one team meeting in which he had been in Fire mode, and went directly into another with a junior colleague who needed to inform him of a family health issue. My client noticed himself holding onto the embers of Fire, assertively instructing the other person. He chose to turn the flame down, and lead with more Water energy, leaning in, listening empathically, and asking what he could do to help.

Leading from Earth

All people have a need for security, for a consistent, grounded element they can trust and rely upon. In our fast-moving world, we risk losing our groundedness, and becoming lost, like a ship in a storm. We need a compass, and stars by which we can steer. It is not only our policies and procedures that ground us, but also our values and mission. At times, leadership can feel breathless. When I teach leaders to centre, they slow down, and start to sense space and stability.

We need to earth ourselves and other people when we are possessed by the Fire and Air of a new idea, and need to test it in a way that we can measure the results, and consider the impact on others, on wider social, social and economic systems, and on the planet itself. Action begins with a first step on the ground, not in the air. Can you bring Earth when needed, when the atmosphere is hot and heady, not to smother an idea, but to harness excitement into grounded, concrete action?

Leading from Air

Within groups, projects and organizations, especially as they mature along their life cycle, energy can start to stagnate and ossify, and a breath of fresh air is needed – new ideas, approaches and ways of doing. Nothing in nature stays the same, and people and organizations that are open to change and able to innovate are more sustainable and resilient.

Leaders need to remain sensitive to points of stagnation within themselves and their organizations, for the latter reflects the former.

When we lead from Air, we tune into the energy around us, and develop our abilities to read shifts and changes, whether on a team, or on an organizational, social, technological or global level. What are you sensing in the energy field? Within the field of energy created by a team or relationship, what is trying to happen? If you tap into this, how can you create something new?

If there is one practice all the leaders with whom I have worked need more of, it is taking time off from day-to-day demands to sense into what's happening in the world around them, and to dream the big picture, create and strategize. Often as a coach, I give people permission to do something they yearn for. One creative director with whom I worked was so busy managing that he rarely connected with his own leadership creativity. I gave him permission to put down his phone, get out of the office, head out into nature, visit galleries and draw again, to replenish his creative well.

Creative energy draws from deep springs of emotional, intellectual and spiritual reserves. When we let these springs dry up, or block their flow, we feel empty and uninspired. All of us need creative energy to see new possibilities and opportunities, and to renew ourselves, our leadership, and our projects and organizations. So much of what we consider time management is actually energy management. When is your best time of day to have ideas? Can you use your Fire and Earth elements to hold boundaries around this time to connect with Air, rather than packing it with more emails and meetings? We can get stuck in a short-term drive for productivity, feel guilty for what we erroneously label 'slacking-off', and push away unstructured, open space for big, blue-sky thinking. But this is not a 'nice-to-have'; it is essential to leadership.

Leading from Water

The leader-as-coach embodies Water energy. You listen, encourage, support and empower. People disengage when they are not seen as people, but as objects and instruments (we'll explore this more fully in the next chapter).

In nature, water is both a binding and a flowing element. Water energy is essential for collaboration. You will face issues you cannot manage alone, so being open and willing to connect with others holds the potential for synergies and partnerships. In top-down leadership structures, I encounter people managing up and down the chain, but rarely looking at who is beside them, especially in siloed organizations (organizations with separate hierarchical teams). One of my clients, a leader in elite sports, felt lonely, with no one at her level to whom she could turn. We decided to look outside her industry for a thinking partner, who faced the same

leadership issues. With whom could you connect? As a leader, Water energy communicates 'We', rather than 'I' – such as, not just bringing people in, but also giving them due credit.

Leading the Energy of Others
By noticing the preferred energies of others, we can also respond to them in a way that helps everyone release their potential. Appreciate the energy that people bring, and meet them where they are initially, if possible.

Fire Someone with a lot of Fire can seem impatient, uncollegiate and argumentative. But we need their energy. If you lead people like this, give them challenges and actionable projects. Level them with Earth, for instance giving them contracts and clear steps, and Air, to help them see the humourous side of their drive. Don't take what can come across as brusqueness personally; they appreciate clear direction and goals. They can burn out with too many demands, so encourage centring and rest to mitigate stress and their tendency to treat everything as urgent and put people's backs up.

Earth If you don't appreciate the element of Earth, those who embody it may seem to be stuffy and officious blockers, rather than enablers. I have worked with several legal counsels and production managers, roles that typically demand a large amount of Earth energy. They look at an idea and ask how they can make it work within existing legal, technological and material constraints. It's not easy being the person who slows a process down for detailed due diligence and problem-solving. But a cut corner can be a sharp edge that causes problems further down the line. The need for Earth creates bottlenecks, and Earth-led, process people can be loaded with heavy and myriad demands. If you lack this element, step into these people's shoes and see the situation from their point of view. Respect and publicly honour their work – they are often unsung heroes.

Air To lead someone with a lot of Air, give them opportunities to create and innovate. Air people are often great initiators, but not always great on detail. Make sure they collaborate with people who can work out a plan to make their ideas happen and who can follow through. In the final chapter, I outline the Three Rooms creative process, which can help focus raw ideas into actionable projects (see page 133).

Water Recognize those around you who hold a strong Water element, and give them the opportunity to grow and thrive. Build relationships and talk with them, rather than issuing emails and directives. They appreciate the personal touch and someone who empathizes with them. As well as in formal groups and meetings, so much energy flows in informal connections in corridors, by the coffee machine, and in the few minutes before the business begins, as people gather. Never discount the value of this and the people who bring warmth and generate camaraderie. One leader in a school was censured by a new principal for spending a few minutes a day

stopping to say hello to the administrative staff, with the rigid injunction, 'It's not your job, and you're not getting paid to chat.' The principal missed entirely that a good trusting relationship between parts of the system, built on those chats, not only encouraged people to feel happier at work – which in itself creates positive energy – but also helped people work well together when problems arose.

LEADERSHIP SHADOW

Because of their impact on people and the world, leaders cast a long and deep shadow. Part of this is influenced by what we keep in shadow about ourselves from ourselves: those unconscious attitudes, biases, beliefs and behaviours that we don't want to see. It takes courageous, honest, ongoing work to manage them, but if you don't, you risk doing more harm than good.

WHEN YOU BECOME A LEADER, you step into the spotlight and intend to bring all your finest qualities into the light with you. Yet, there are unconscious qualities and energies you also carry, which may profoundly affect your leadership. The mind comes with a built-in mechanism to protect the ego with favourable images of ourselves, which screen our messy tendencies and feelings of pain and shame. No one is perfect. We all have vulnerabilities and insecurities. That powerful defence mechanism works furiously to deny the truth to ourselves. What it hides is our shadow. Poor leaders recreate their own ego-defences in the choice of people they surround themselves with. They don't like someone holding up a mirror that reflects back that which they cannot bear to see about themselves. They become intolerant of dissent, and people hold back from offering it. Unable to own their own less-desirable tendencies, they project them onto others, for instance, believing others to be untrustworthy, when they themselves are insincere. They fear the truth being revealed. The fragile truce between what they want to believe about themselves, and the more complicated human reality creates a faultline in their leadership.

We cannot be a thoughtful leader without an ongoing commitment to expand awareness of our shadow and its impact. The problem in leadership is that the negative tendencies to which we are blind are often glaringly obvious to others. The Johari window is a psychological model that frames this. The window has four quadrants:

A good leader is intensely aware of the
interplay of inner shadow and light, lest the act of
leadership do more harm than good.

PARKER J. PALMER (1939–)
FOUNDER AND SENIOR PARTNER EMERITUS
OF THE CENTER FOR COURAGE AND RENEWAL

- The Open Self: what you and others know about you.
- The Hidden Self: what you know, but others don't.
- The Blind Self: what others know about you, but you don't.
- The Unknown Self: what neither you nor others are aware of.

The Blind Self area, where your unconscious shadow affects others, requires your acceptance (we all have blind spots), and ongoing attention to keep as small as possible.

Self-Acceptance

True self-acceptance is acceptance of ourselves at our least acceptable. That includes accepting, rather than rejecting or denying, our shadows: those 'unacceptable' parts of ourselves, such as our capacity to get things wrong, and the fact we are not very nice or reasonable at times.

My shadow includes a know-it-all tendency, of which I can be in denial, as it doesn't fit with my preferred self-image of compassion. As a newly promoted leader in the corporate realm, I used to shoot down my team's ideas before they finished speaking. Eventually, when I called upon my team to come up with ideas, the room would fall silent. I blinded myself to the effect my shadow was having, because I didn't want to accept I could act in such a way, so I blamed others for being lazy. If good leadership unleashes others' potential, then I was failing. By owning and accepting my tendency to be an ideas assassin, I can notice when my shadow takes over.

Managing Shadow

What helps us manage the influence and impact of shadow? Therapy is a good start to build awareness and acceptance, and I recommend leaders have a professional with whom they can talk confidentially on a regular basis. In addition, here are some suggestions of day-to-day practices.

Self-Care

Managing shadow will be easier on a good day, than on a bad day. Twelve-step programmes, such as Alcoholics Anonymous, have an acronym, H.A.L.T., to help people notice when they are entering the danger zone, in which someone is more likely to reach for the bottle, call their dealer or take their credit card for a spin. When you are Hungry, Angry, Lonely or Tired, your negative tendencies have the perfect environment in which to run amok. Notice your own personal danger zones and integrate self-care as a leadership practice. For instance, when I haven't meditated or stretched, when I haven't had meaningful connection with people and nature for a few days, before my first cup of tea, and when I am stressed, then my shadow can emerge. Get familiar with the circumstances that push you into the danger zone.

Emotional Literacy

The second step to manage shadow as much as possible is to develop emotional literacy. Expand your emotional vocabulary to acknowledge your feelings: you might discern that you are not *angry* at someone for missing a deadline, but *disappointed* and *lonely*, feeling that no one else understands. Spend time with yourself when you feel strong emotions, instead of trying to suppress them by avoidance strategies, such as reaching for distractions. The ability to bear uncomfortable feelings is a hallmark of emotional maturity and thoughtful leadership. Notice how that sensation feels in your body. Ask that part of you that is suffering what it needs from the perspective of your Inner Ally, or your wise, compassionate and courageous self.

In our fast-paced, ever-changing environment, developing emotional awareness is crucial, takes time and courage, builds resilience and empathy, and relieves stress. We reduce the risk of casting our shadow onto others, and blaming others for our feelings. When we can accept this about ourselves, we are more likely to accept vulnerabilities in others.

Feedback

Finally, encourage feedback. Feedback can be uncomfortable to receive and to give, so create psychological safety for the person from whom you want feedback. Be specific: for instance, say, 'I would be grateful if you could let me know how you think I come across in tomorrow's meeting, as I feel I am cutting people off', rather than 'Am I a good leader?' Ask about leadership blind spots, as others will be more aware of them than you. Common examples are insensitivity, blaming others, avoiding difficult conversations, gossiping and going behind people's backs, and being casual about commitments such as meetings. If you notice a reaction to any of these, it might be a place for you to investigate.

Be grateful for any feedback you receive and show you are listening. People have basic emotional needs (more on this in the next chapter), and being listened to, acknowledged and valued are at the top of the list.

Acknowledging Wounds

There is one more place into which I want us to venture with courage, honesty and compassion. In the first chapter, I asked you to consider your story. Somewhere in there is the crucible of your leadership. It may not be a place of joy; it can just as well be a wound. Many leaders don't acknowledge their woundedness, and this causes damage. Their leadership can be a great howl into the world – a desire to control and command in the hope of ending pain. A wound can generate a great amount of energy.

Buddhists talk of the hungry ghost: the figure who tries to fill themselves on that which does not nourish them, accepting a substitute that never truly satisfies. As a coach, for instance, I need to take care that I am not supporting others to avoid my own issues. When I notice that I am trying to feed myself by taking on too much responsibility for the feelings or

progress of my clients, I centre and let it go with compassion. I fail regularly. I pick myself up each time and reset, choosing not to let shame overwhelm me. I am human, and doing my best. I have had and continue to have coaches, therapists, friends and a community that see me and compassionately call me forth to do better. I recommend you do the same.

We detect the echo of our woundedness when we ache to belong to the 'in' group, to impress others, and fear their rejection, desiring to feel accepted, admired and loved. Do not seek love through leadership, for you feed the hungry ghost. It will never be enough, not for long. You'll strive to have more, control more, please more, and you'll destroy yourself, your relationships, your organizations and the planet in the process.

Heal yourself by loving yourself. First, be aware of your woundedness, and how it shows up in your life and leadership. The next step is commitment to ongoing therapy with a professional psychotherapist. You may also find conscious women's and men's group work helpful. The ongoing leadership path is to commit every day to noticing, accepting and choosing, and that means picking yourself up with compassion and resetting. It takes emotional courage to be a thoughtful leader. You are not alone.

CHAPTER FOUR

LEADING
WITH AWARENESS
OF OTHERS

The notion of separateness is an illusion.
Leaders are not alone. We lead mutually
interdependent ecosystems, within which we have
impact, connection and alliances. When we
intentionally foster an ethos with emotional and social
intelligence, we sow trust, and co-create environments
in which we, our partnerships, teams, organizations
and communities can thrive. After leading ourselves,
the next step on the path of thoughtful leadership is
giving conscious consideration to leading others.

THINKING IN SYSTEMS

We can't talk about leadership without considering those who follow. Leadership can conjure the illusion of separateness. Yet, we are all part of webs of connection, which we can influence for good or for ill.

As a leader, you may sometimes *feel* alone and separate, but it doesn't mean you *are* so. As humans, we are wedded to an erroneous sense of self. Leaders who cling to this sense of self cause suffering to themselves, to others, and ultimately to the world and its ecosystems. When it comes to leading others, thoughtful leaders know separateness is an illusion. Your greatest resource is and will always be people, regardless of your endeavour. People who care about what they do will be more energized, positive, focused and creative. They want to self-actualize, and it's your role to appreciate this and create the environment in which they can.

Yet the vast majority of people worldwide are not engaged in their work, and those who lead them account for 70 percent of the variance in engagement, according to a 2017 Gallup poll. If leaders make the difference, then something is not working, and this is as true in the workplace as it is in the political sphere, as well as in my own field of self-development, where disillusionment with teachers on ethical grounds has become a feature.

I believe part of the problem lies in how we relate to each other. So much of our interaction with those around us is transactional, instrumental and top-down, and this impoverishes the potential of our leadership, and of those we lead. In this chapter, we'll explore some of the ways leaders can change this for the good of all, by immersing in one of the currents of the river of reality – our hard-wired need for connection to each other.

Open & Closed Systems

I invite you to think of yourself and others not as discrete individuals, but holistically, as parts of a system: sets of interdependent participants with a common focus or identity, all influencing each other in a dynamic, energetic field. The power of the whole is greater than the sum of the individuals within it, which is why collaboration has birthed great social, cultural, technological, economic, political and spiritual achievements.

We are like islands

in the sea, separate on the surface but

connected in the deep.

WILLIAM JAMES (1842–1910)
AMERICAN PHILOSOPHER AND FATHER OF AMERICAN PSYCHOLOGY

MINDFULNESS EXERCISE

TUNING IN

In the overstimulation of our everyday lives, we can pull our attention inwards to prevent feeling overwhelmed. The practice of tuning into our senses takes us out of our heads and back into the world.

1 You can practise this sitting, standing or walking. Initially, I recommend practising at a time you won't be disturbed.

2 Centre yourself. Take at least one minute for each of the steps below.

3 Start to become aware of your hands. Slowly rub your fingertips over whatever they are touching. Take in the detail of texture, temperature and shape.

4 Next, bring your attention to the furthest sound you can hear and focus on it for a minute. Then, switch your attention to the closest sound.

5 If your eyes are closed, open them. Pay close attention to one area that you can see, as if you have never seen anything like it before. Then, switch to a more diffused peripheral vision, by defocusing on that area and becoming gently aware of what's in the space around you.

6 Bring your attention to your breath. Focus on the sensation and temperature of air as you inhale through the nostrils. After a minute, switch your attention to the rise and fall of your chest. If you can, focus on the up-and-down movement of your ribs for one breath, back-and-front for the next, and finally, side-to-side expansion. Now drop your attention to your belly and notice it move as you breathe.

7 This last part takes some practice, so don't give up or blame yourself if it isn't easy at first. Slowly expand your awareness to include what is close to you: the surface your weight is on, your clothes, and then objects close to you. Now, hold that awareness and extend it outwards to include more of the environment around you. What can you hold in your field of awareness? I recommend all leaders get into the habit of practising extended awareness by holding two 'tracks' simultaneously – awareness of themselves, and awareness of others and what's going on around them – or switching mindfully between the two.

We also need to bring mindful awareness to the type of system we lead. Is it closed or open? A closed system is like a watch: interactions occur only among its elements. Rigid boundaries restrict the flow of information and energy in and out, with stagnation and entropy the eventual result, unless external energy revitalizes it. An open system is like a tree: connected to its wider ecology, continually receiving input, and sending output back. It evolves as a result of exchanges with its environment: stimulation creates adaptation and renewal. A system open to learning, committed to growth, flexible rather than defensive, and responsive rather than reactive will be more effective and resilient. Creating and sustaining an open system is the ongoing responsibility of a leader, in partnership with everyone else.

Systems have an innate wisdom that leaders can tap into to influence, support, regulate, nurture and lead. The most powerful way we affect them is not by willing others to change, but by changing ourselves, and so transforming the dynamic. In this chapter, we're going to look at the system in which we lead others, and discover how to influence it positively and release the potential of its wisdom and power.

YOUR IMPACT

You bring your whole self to thoughtful leadership, and see others as whole as well. We all bring emotional needs and ghosts from old systems with us, which need to be understood, acknowledged and accepted, even if it means dispelling a few leadership myths.

IMAGINE THAT YOU — along with everyone else — carry an invisible array of the many systems to which you belong or have belonged: family, relationships, previous employment or involvement with organizations, leadership experiences, education, social and cultural systems. From these old systems, we bring emotional needs and ghosts. By limiting ourselves to transactional relationships and exchanges, we cut ourselves off from wider understanding of what energizes our systems, and from deeper connection with other people. Emotional needs and ghosts don't simply ask us to clear them: they are sources of energy and potential, and a wise and thoughtful leader creates the trust and connection through which their positive power arises anew in every moment.

Here's an enduring leadership myth: to be successful, you leave your emotions at the door. This is naïve at best and thwarts great leadership at worst. In every system, everyone — including the leader — has emotional needs they seek to be met. From birth, we tune into the emotional weather around us for reassuring signs these needs can be met. As a leader, followers primarily look to you for this, and we are also seeking the same from them. Thoughtful leaders – aware and unafraid of their own and other's emotional needs – acknowledge them directly or indirectly. This prism explains some of the apparently irrational behaviour between leaders and followers. When someone comes to you with an issue, are they seeking a solution, or acknowledgment? If you offer them the former without the latter, you haven't addressed the emotional need behind the request and, even with the best of intentions, can end up disappointing and disengaging them.

Emotional Needs

We all have emotional needs. Here are a few pertinent ones for leaders to understand.

- Safety – 'Can I trust?'
- Acknowledgment – 'Am I seen?'
- Belonging – 'Am I included?'
- Appreciation – 'Am I valued?'
- Usefulness – 'Am I making a contribution?'
- Challenge – 'Am I learning and growing?'
- Meaning – 'Why do I care? Why do I matter?'
- Purpose – 'Do I know why I am here?'

Transference

Why do people look to get their emotional needs met by a leader? If the first question of leadership is 'Why do you want to lead?', then the second is, 'Why do people want to follow you?' From a transactional, material perspective, they want status, occupation, payment, experience and skills. But from a systems perspective, which includes emotional needs and ghosts, people's motivations arise from the powerful unconscious images and emotions that we all transfer onto our relationships with leaders.

Sigmund Freud, the founder of psychoanalysis, observed that a significant number of his patients fell in love with him. Setting aside the charms and fascination of his couch-side manner, he realized that people were relating to him as if he was an important person from their past – usually a parent. This 'transference', in which people carry across emotions from past relationships onto present ones, is activated between leaders and followers like ghosts in the machine. Followers project their unconscious desire to have their emotional needs met onto you, because, in psychotherapeutic terms, you are the parent-substitute. Yet, they are also ambivalent towards the 'parent' who represents both the promise of satisfaction and the fear of denial, rejection or punishment. More than once, a frustrated leader has unconsciously detected this ghost, complaining to me, 'I am not their mum or dad!'

To illustrate this, let me introduce you to two parent archetypes. The 'stern' parent humiliates, bullies and threatens; the 'indulgent' parent disempowers. As leaders, we amplify and accentuate the power of the ghost by inhabiting one of these parent roles. Our harsh judgment and scornful impatience increase pain and torment by infantilizing the other person, stripping them of dignity and self-respect. On the other hand, when we coddle people, we train them into childish learned helplessness.

Transference can work positively and negatively. Thoughtful leaders don't buy into their followers' idealized and glorified images of them. But even leaders who are reasonably self-aware can take the occasional dip in the river of illusion. The 'halo effect' of being 'loved' is seductive and energizing. How do you feel when people think that because you said something, it must be right? At the other end of the scale, the 'horn effect' of being demonized or 'hated' can throw you into recrimination of yourself and others, and armouring ('Who cares? I'm not here to be loved'). Followers can feel deep disappointment, defeat, hurt or even rage when you do not acknowledge or accept their needs, and may release that negative and harmful energy, grumbling about you. While it might be true that a leader is not there to be loved, consider the emotional capital you have to get things done when people feel positive and energized around you, even when you have to say no.

A Coaching Story: The Boundaried Leader

One of my clients was exhausted by people coming to her all day with problems. But her own leadership behaviour was responsible. To change the behaviour of others, she had to change her own, and stop acting unconsciously like an indulgent parent, saying yes to all comers, and 'fixing' issues they could have solved themselves. When we worked together to own her emotional needs, she realized she was hooked on fixing problems, in order to meet her own need for feeling useful and validated.

She needed to move into conscious action by asserting boundaries. But saying 'No, sort it yourself' felt inauthentic and aggressive to her, so we found a script with which she felt comfortable: 'I would like to help, but I can't sit down with you until next Wednesday.' At which point most of her followers usually went away and found their own solution.

By accepting her responsibility for the system dynamic, and doing her inner work to change her role in it, she transformed it after years of blaming other people and exhausting herself. When someone did have a problem that required her attention, rather than fixing it, she spoke adult-to-adult, and supported them to find their own solutions using coaching skills. She transformed her leadership and her team, by unhooking them all.

Empowering People

Former US President Barack Obama once said that only the really hard problems came to his desk, as the smaller ones were dealt with further down the chain of command. That tells me he had empowered his team. Many of my leadership clients sometimes vent their frustration with the amount of time they spend putting out small fires, when they want to work on the bigger issues. This may be a sign they are in the systemic parent role interpersonally and organizationally. Notice when you slip into parent-child relations (and you can regress into the child state too, even as a leader), have compassion for yourself and the other person or people, and consciously choose to relate as an adult.

Apart from our skilfulness in self-awareness and self-management, we can reduce the level and impact of parent-child transference in a system, whether with a person or a group, by staying aware, empowering them, holding boundaries and resisting unconscious collusion. When one person in a relationship system unconsciously behaves like a parent, the other person is more likely to behave as a child, and vice versa.

◆

Treat people as if they were what they ought to be, and you help them become what they are capable of being.

JOHANN WOLFGANG VON GOETHE (1749–1832)
GERMAN WRITER AND STATESMAN

◆

Emotional Maturity

Leaders need to mindfully demonstrate emotional maturity to thwart transference. The traits of an emotionally mature person are also those of thoughtful leaders:

- Taking responsibility
- Showing empathy
- Owning mistakes
- Being unafraid of vulnerability
- Recognizing and accepting needs
- Setting healthy boundaries
- Identifying and managing emotions
- Pausing between feeling and reacting
- Practising self-control and delaying instant gratification

Once these traits are our own, we can encourage them within others who want to be valued by us. With our leadership power to influence the system, the world will experience its rewards.

Leadership is relational and active. Your impact will be unconsciously affected by systemic dynamics and transferences in the emotional field. When we ignore or avoid them, we fail to lead thoughtfully. Even when we say we leave our emotions at the door, few of us can, nor should we want to.

YOUR CONNECTION

◆

In the first chapters, we made more conscious and deepened the connection we have with ourselves. The next step on the leadership path requires attention to our connection with others. The quality and effectiveness of our leadership reflects the quality of the rich emotional connection forged with attentive presence.

W HAT DO YOU BELIEVE is the most valuable tool for leading others? Your knowledge, your vision, your determination, your wit? It is simpler than that: the answer lies in your attentive presence. Whatever the situation in front of you, when you give people attentive presence, you'll find resolution closer than when you withhold it. Yet it is one of the hardest gifts to give because it requires you to slow down and tune in, made harder still by an environment which entrains us to speed up, do more, distract and multi-task.

Attentive presence is the core of emotional connection, and connection is the channel through which thoughtful leadership flows. The prerequisites of attentive presence are courage, curiosity and empathy, and its practice is deep listening. Courage to experience, identify and name our feelings and to ask after another's; curiosity about our own and others' emotions; and empathy to attend to mutual differences. Approach other people with, at some level, a certain wonder and bring that with you in your leadership system.

How to Listen Deeply

When we give attentive presence to someone, showing interest without interruption or judgment, we create trust and empowerment. But we need to stay aware of what we are listening to. Are we listening to the other person, or to ourselves?

When we listen to ourselves, although we might hear the words of another, our attention is on what these words mean to us personally. For instance, we might be thinking, 'I know the answer', 'This person is getting on my nerves' or 'I wonder how the meeting is going to go later'. When we notice we are listening to ourselves, we compassionately nudge ourselves out of this state to listen to someone else.

When we listen deeply to another person, we listen to their words and notice their body language, without over-interpreting it. We notice their energy, words they stress or repeat and their expressions. We also enquire with curiosity, using powerful questions that evoke clarity, discovery, insight and action. Once people receive this level of attention, they can often find their own solutions.

Attention is the rarest and purest form of generosity.

SIMONE WEIL (1909–43)
PHILOSOPHER AND POLITICAL ACTIVIST

The Emotional Work of Leadership

When avoidance of true, human connection becomes our default, the inner muscle that tones up through emotional work atrophies. Transactional, top-down, command-and-control interactions may feel safer and easier, but lose something precious and they won't help you release the potential in others, which is the point of leadership. Attentive presence and emotional connection require energy. Often, that's what makes us avoid them. It can feel like yet another tax on our time and emotions. It doesn't have to be; a five-minute conversation can be meaningful. But it's difficult to set aside what you're doing, disengage from your screen, and focus on the person you're with. Usually when you do that, the other person will feel the connection, and respond in kind.

We are not helped by the famine of attention brought about by our reliance on electronic communication. All day, we're caught in an overwhelming blizzard of emails, messaging, social media posts, unable to be present with ourselves or another, all the while starving for real connection. Our distraction by and reliance on electronic communication depends upon our brain's attraction to it (a fact its designers exploit), because, as we explored in chapter two (see page 46), the mind will automatically wander, even without an infernal machine tempting us. How often, when you are supposed to be listening to someone, are you actually planning what you are going to say next, or wondering if that email has arrived? Moment to moment we lose ourselves, and disconnect from our own and others' emotions.

Curiosity & Humility

Leaders who fail to tune in to what's happening within and around them turn off others, and are blind to important signals. It takes courage to lean into our senses during a difficult conversation, for instance: to witness and name without judgment what we are feeling in a given moment, and to take responsibility and own it, rather than blame someone else. Often, we try to hide our emotions, even from ourselves, and so may be even more prone to blindspots, knee-jerk reactions and unconscious biases. It takes courage and curiosity to ask about another's emotions.

If, as leaders, we use our time with people solely to issue directives, we lose the opportunity for connection. The leadership switch can get jammed in 'tell' mode, if we believe lack of knowledge is a sign of weakness, or fear that we will be overwhelmed by others' needs. We don't know everything, and we need the input and wisdom of others. The art of asking, rather than telling; being curious, rather than assuming, takes courage. As well as building adult-to-adult connection and trust, we need to hear about problems, and create the psychological safety for people to respond honestly. We do this by managing our responses rather than reacting, engaging in deep listening and showing that we are human and mess up too. When we encourage candour when things aren't going well, we can elicit ideas to improve them. When we follow up, people know we listened, so we need to ask them how they will know we have done so. When we have a better idea of the issues people face, what they care about and how they recognize connection, we can imaginatively see the world from their point of view, and it's the ability to empathize that builds trust.

Conflict

We have already explored how we change our own states and patterns, consciously regulating and shaping them with awareness, acceptance and choice. When we do, we have the most profound and positive influence on others in the system. This is the essence of emotional intelligence. Emotions are contagious. Stress and negativity spread like a virus, and any part of the system can infect parts or the whole. Peace and positivity also travel the same interconnected threads. It is our task as leaders to be aware of and manage our inner stress reactions, as we will sometimes deal with the stress of others, and inevitably, with conflict.

MINDFULNESS EXERCISE

LEADING DIFFICULT CONVERSATIONS

Practising this exercise tones your ability to skilfully facilitate conflict for the benefit of all.

1 Think of a recent difficult conversation you wish you had handled better. Replay it objectively as if a film camera had been running. What were the concrete, observable actions? For example, 'You told me you hadn't completed the project.'

2 What were the physical sensations and emotions you experienced? For instance, 'My chest tightened. I felt frustrated and angry.'

3 Why did this matter to you? Be transparent about what you valued and needed, for example, 'I value transparency and reliability, and need to know I can trust and depend on you.'

4 What would you like to request in the form of a concrete offer to help fulfil this need? A request is something someone can say no to without fear of reprisal or heavy cost. There are three types of requests: clarity, feedback and action. For instance, 'I would like to ask you if you would be willing to tell me what happened from your point of view?'

Once you have practised this, you will be able to call on this process the next time conflict arises. Rather than being overtaken by stress, leaping to interpretations, assumptions and blame or victimhood, follow this process with open curiosity and compassion, starting with observations, then feelings, needs, and finally requests. Be transparent about the process, and teach it to others as part of your agreement, alliance or organizational culture. This will create connection and trust, and ultimately flow through conflict, rather than being hooked on judgment and suffering.

Conflict is not only inevitable, but welcome in certain circumstances lest partnerships or teams fall into groupthink, which is not the best, stress-tested thinking. But at times of stress and conflict, our best intentions and emotional maturity can be overridden by our automatic survival reactions in an instant. Our beliefs about and attitudes towards conflict require honest scrutiny. What is your typical reaction to conflict? Use the five stress reaction patterns we explored in chapter two as a guide (see page 42). For instance, I have a strong freeze-and-flight pattern when conflict arises and I can regress to the state I was as a small child, hearing my parents arguing – not very useful in my life and work today. As a leader, the importance of awareness, acceptance and choice is paramount. Once we can unwind our automatic reactions, we have space to discern how we want to deal with conflict.

One way is to apply curiosity, rather than create story. What is trying to emerge? For example, people often argue about unmet emotional needs, how they communicate or about role clarity, even though it may seem they are arguing about something else: 'I was kept out of the loop' or 'You overstepped the mark'. So, the opportunity here is to see how needs can be met, communication can be improved or roles clarified (I suggest ways to facilitate this in the section on 'Your Alliance' later in this chapter – see page 110). Ask the system by asking people within it what needs to happen. If we avoid conflict, we can't transform it.

Many relationships deepen when conflict is skilfully facilitated, and this depends on maintaining our connection even
in a hot spot. When someone withdraws connection, emotional needs aren't acknowledged, trust erodes and
relationships wither. The most valuable guide we have for this
comes from fields such as Non-Violent Communication. What
we value in all relationships, perhaps most especially in conflict, is compassion. As we have touched upon preiously,
compassion connects us to each other as human beings. When
we close our hearts, we withdraw emotional connection.
Leaders are prized for finding solutions to conflict, but in
relationships, we value our connection to each other, even if
we cannot agree. We will inevitably at times lose it in the heat
of an argument, so forgive yourself, and consciously recover
your connection with the other person or people with honesty and humility. When we treat other people as worthy of
value and importance – as ends in themselves, rather than
simply as means – it colours how we are with them, and thus
how they feel and respond. We grant dignity and self-respect
to us and them.

Heart-set & Mindset

A leader's own inner emotional work is vital to their effec-
tiveness. We need to check our heart-set and mindset. When
we operate from a view of ourselves as right and important,
deserving and entitled, needing to be well-thought of,

thwarted and unappreciated, or broken and deficient, we risk creating ongoing suffering and the response that will continue to feed it. When we can meet resistance not with equal and opposite resistance, or by collapsing into victimhood and blaming, but centred with curiosity and openness, we'll affect the system positively.

A poor leader sees people as objects – obstacles, vehicles, instruments and irrelevancies. A thoughtful leader sees people as people, with their own needs, values, desires and insecurities – just like them. This recognition builds our connection. We may seem to be separate, yet in reality we are deeply connected.

Because of your leadership impact, the positive effects of attentive presence and emotional connection allow people to flourish. They feel stimulated and encouraged to think and act in new and creative ways. I love the following example of the power of attentive presence from a leader, with its courage, curiosity and empathy. In preparation for the 2012 London Olympic opening ceremony, director Danny Boyle met the volunteering performers in small groups. He asked them what was important to them about Great Britain, listened, and built a people-centred, heart-lead spectacle. He knew the value of emotional connection. His leadership style explains what made that particular opening ceremony so affecting to me. Everyone was brimming with pride and purpose. I didn't see nameless masses; I saw individuals who cared.

YOUR ALLIANCE

———◆———

As a leader of others, your role is to create an environment within which people can release their fullest potential through being together. As leaders, when we consciously co-create alliances, we generate the conditions in which everyone can thrive.

WHEN WE COME TOGETHER for a project, we typically spend time thinking about *what* we are working on. We rarely consider *how* we want to work together, although it is our awareness of the group as an interdependent system connected and motivated by values that energizes our best efforts. By co-creating an alliance between everyone, built on asking and listening, values-in-action, responsibility, commitment and accountability on all sides, the system sees itself and how it works best. A healthy system supports, nurtures and cares for the wellbeing of everyone. Reveal the system to itself, and take time to consciously co-create it with its members as a transforming, open, thriving entity.

In an alliance, everyone has awareness of the roles they play, and takes responsibility for them. Rather than making assumptions, we consciously co-create and commit to a set of behavioural norms and processes, and pay attention to how the system is working. For instance, you will need concrete behavioural agreements around communication, respect, managing conflict and making decisions. It's a living contract, so you can also redesign it at any time or for particular contexts, such as during a period of stress or change.

The Team Perspective

A great partnership or team is more than the sum of its parts. In designing an alliance, personal perspectives and needs are important, but the perspective of the team, organization and purpose can get lost. The key question in the design is, 'What does this *team or partnership* need to thrive?' When we work and live in silos, our view narrows. The partnership or team system is bigger than any one person or function. In meetings where I have facilitated teams to design their alliance, I keep a chair empty, explaining that it holds the perspective of the team. I offer an open invitation for anyone at any time to sit in the chair, and speak from the perspective of the team. It moves people out of siloed thinking.

Agreeing Roles

By paying conscious attention to your alliance for each project, you can bring some clarity around roles and responsibilities by using the RACI model. For each project, agree the following: Who is Responsible? Who is Accountable? Who is Consulted? Who is Informed?

I once worked with a leadership team who were unclear on roles, which resulted in people stepping on each other's toes, and the CEO taking too much responsibility. After applying

A Coaching Story: The Team Alliance

Sudha and Meghan (not their real names) founded a successful creative agency, and recruited Ash as their first senior manager. The co-founders asked me to facilitate an alliance-making session on a morning out of the office.

I started by asking, 'What does your relationship need to thrive?'

'Empathy', said Ash.

'Great, what does that look like in action?'

'When I feel that others understand when my workload is full.'

'How would you know that others understand?'

'When I can tell them without fear, and we work together for a solution.'

I turned to the others, 'Can you agree to this?'

Sudha murmured, 'Well…'

I paused, remaining open and curious. Something wanted to emerge here and it was important to let it.

'Our clients are demanding, and our reputation is built upon being able to service their needs, or they'll go elsewhere. Sometimes you have to suck it up. I can't ask our juniors to work late if we aren't.'

'I hear you,' I acknowledged, 'Thank you for being honest. Knowing that both of you have these needs, how do you feel right now?'

Sudha was worried, Ash ambivalent.

'What would you like to request of each other and what can you commit to?'

Ash responded, 'I would like to feel that my need to have boundaries around my family time is respected.'

'And what would that look like?'

'I would like a discussion before I work over a weekend.'

'OK, Sudha and Meghan, can you agree to that?'

'Sure,' Sudha said, 'I'd be happy to. Can Ash listen to our reasons and let us know if he feels frustrated. I don't want him to feel he can't talk to us and end up leaving.'

'So I hear a need for trust and honest communication here, shall I add this to the contract?'

'Yes!' they said.

A few months later I met them again to see how things had been going. Their agreement built trust and positivity into the team, with benefits for their enterprise.

the RACI model, tension eased as people were clear on how to work together, leadership shifted when appropriate, people carried their own weight and respected each other.

MOTIVATING OTHERS

Motivation is the driving force behind our greatest achievements. Thoughtful leaders understand what really motivates people. When they help people to feel motivated, it's an act of love, which releases their potential and creates positive results.

YOUR ALARM GOES OFF on Monday morning. You think of your day ahead. What feelings break through the morning fog? Motivation is the difference between waking up excited about your day, and dragging yourself out of bed with a heavy heart. It is key to unleashing potential and realizing our greatest achievements.

Emotions play a powerful role in motivation. Today and in the future, more of the people you lead are seeking fulfilment through work and being involved in organizations, communities and movements. To what extent are you facilitating this? Are you fostering commitment or compliance, through love or fear (including fear of loss of material incentives or reputation)? While coercive or extrinsically incentivizing leaders might motivate people in the short-term, the long-term cost is huge in terms of engagement, stress, loyalty and potential.

Don't let the temptation of short-term gains outweigh the benefits of long-term focus.

Intrinsic Motivation

We explored in chapter one how intrinsic values, rather than extrinsic incentives such as bonuses or threat of redundancy, motivate you and everyone around you in the long-term (see page 24). Understanding that has implications for our leadership. Instead of assuming people will be motivated by the same things you are, use the 'Values-in-Action' exercise in chapter one (see page 28) to uncover the values of those you lead. When they are driven by intrinsic values, people deploy different and more creative learning strategies – those that demand more effort, and enable them to process information more deeply. They also prefer tasks that are more challenging, and are willing to put in greater amounts of effort to achieve goals over the long haul. If creativity motivates someone, give them the opportunity to develop it, not just in what they do, but in how they tackle problems. If challenge lights them up, work with them to set meaningful ones that help them grow, rather than allow them to get bored.

Understanding Motivation

As well as taking the time to understand the intrinsic values that energize people, thoughtful leaders should consider certain universal values that evidence suggests are important in people feeling they are fulfilling their potential. These are:

Freedom Show people you trust them. Involve them in decision-making, particularly when they will be directly affected by the decision.

Meaning Help people see and feel how they make a difference. Ask them what would make what they do meaningful.

Challenge Many people want to develop their skills or knowledge. Good leaders offer progression, stretch goals and continually enrich roles in duties, responsibilities and accountability, while at the same time instilling confidence that the challenges can be met.

Mastery People like to get better at things. Are you giving people the support they need to get really good at something?

Acknowledgment and appreciation Show people you value them. Engagement is a direct reflection of how people feel about their relationship with you. Take time to make personal connections with people, avoid favouritism, and credit ideas and effort as well as results.

Not everyone will be motivated by the same combination of these values, so I recommend you ask rather than assume.

Making It Personal

People aren't inspired by what you do, they are inspired by why you do it, so share your purpose. Make it personal and authentic. Show them what you have discovered on your leadership path. Share why you became a leader, and the difference

you want to make in the world with them. Create a space in which people share what matters to them, how they see their purpose, and how it works together with the partnership or team purpose.

One of the privileges of my work as a facilitator is witnessing how the system renews and invigorates itself, when people relate to each other at this level and see each other with new eyes, with a sense of wonder, trust and respect. I see how this renewal lights up a leader in turn. We may not always agree, nor should we wish to, but when we can be clear about what it is we can align with, we create a partnership or team that can weather conflict within and adversity without. We are not separate, ever.

The richness of our leadership and lives is defined by the quality of our relationships with each other, and by the nature of the systems we co-create. All open systems evolve and generate their own energy, which is bigger than you, and if you are truly a great leader, they will continue to do so and flourish after you have gone.

If you want to build a ship, don't drum up the men to gather wood, divide the work and give orders. Instead, teach them to yearn for the vast and endless sea.

ANTOINE DE SAINT-EXUPÉRY (1900–44)
WRITER AND PIONEERING AVIATOR

CHAPTER FIVE

LEADING CULTURE

Leadership comes from the heart: we long for something. It originates from the soul: we connect with something bigger than ourselves. How do you long to make the world a better place? What are you going to leave behind? Our greatest contribution as a leader lies not only in what we materially achieve, but also in the culture we help create, where resilience, creativity, innovation, diversity and inclusion, and sustainability are the norms.

DEEP-TIME LEADERSHIP

◆

What is the difference you want to make in the world, not just in your lifetime, but for what comes after you? Your everyday choices influence the future. Choose wisely and well.

I MAGINE YOU ARE STANDING on the top of a hill on a windy summer's day. You feel the sun on your skin one moment, and the cool breeze the next. At this moment, you are attuned to the weather. Now imagine that you stood on this hill for fifty years, and noticed the changes in the number and intensity of storms as time passes. You're attuned to the climate. Now imagine that, under your feet, you could sense the slow shifting of tectonic plates. If you stood here for a million years, the landscape would look very different. The hill might be on the plain, rivers that don't yet exist might flow through valleys. This is deep time.

Leaders are time travellers: they pay attention to the present, and to their future vision. In taking steps to be a more thoughtful leader, you are creating the conditions for better leadership for generations ahead.

Long-Term Impact

The danger arises when, in the day-to-day demands of leadership, we don't consider the long-term impact of what we do – not just the negative consequences we want to avoid, but

the positive ones we wish to contribute. We focus on winning an argument, rather than building a relationship. We concentrate on improving our yearly results for our shareholder dividends, rather than considering the long-term value of our companies. We think about the press release, rather than culture change. What we are teaching the next generation of leaders will affect leadership culture for years to come.

There are four reasons why thinking long-term is hard. One, as humans, we are tempted by short-term gratification. The ability to delay gratification, and think longer term is a sign of emotional maturity. Many of today's issues are too complex and deep-rooted to be solved quickly. Two, we can be too humble. We say, 'Who am I to make such a difference? I am only one person.' But, as we have seen, you are part of an ecosystem, and your collective contribution makes that difference. Three, we are often motivated by fear of loss, rather than hope of gain. We can see this 'pulling up the ladder' behaviour when leaders protect their own positions. Finally, we lack imagination. Leaders need to keep strengthening their imaginative muscle. They need to dream big and deep.

In this final chapter, we are going to consider the essential leadership question of how we lead the culture, focus on resilience, diversity, inclusion and empowerment, creativity and innovation, prospection, and sustainability and legacy. I offer a few ideas and techniques here, but encourage you to explore more as part of your thoughtful leadership path.

Resilience

◆

All thoughtful leadership is resilient. Change is inevitable, and much of it is out of our control. But we do have control over how we respond. The practices of resilience are not just for action when times are tough, but for every day, to make ourselves better and stronger.

Let me lie to you. Leadership is easy. People are easy. Life is easy. I have the magic pill that will make everything simple and straightforward. You'll be able to have what you want, when you want it, without difficulty or setbacks. You'll have perfect health all your life. No one you love will ever suffer. Every project will meet with success. Life will be fair.

To be honest, I'd like that pill too. That is, until I consider that all my struggles have made me who I am. If I hadn't had to dig myself out of holes, I wouldn't know I could. You need to build a resilient culture, because troubles will come from within and without. The fact that obstacles appear doesn't mean you are failing on the leadership path, because learning how to transcend them *is* the path of thoughtful leadership.

It's a mistake to believe that everything stays the same, that nothing ever changes. Impermanence is the nature of all things. As a leader in any area of life, your attitude or mindset towards change affects the outcome. Do you believe that you can't grow, or that you can learn and adapt? When we notice we are in the former mindstate, we can choose to switch into the latter. Culture also has a mindset, led by you. As a leader, your mind- and heart-set is the template for others and for the culture you create.

Growth from Adversity

After a setback, the majority of people dust themselves off and get back to normal. But a thoughtful leader creates a resilient culture in which people believe that growth emerges from adversity. There's a new normal: stronger, and more creative. Growth from adversity is rarer than coping, and forms the operating belief of thoughtful leadership culture.

Acknowledgment After a setback, the first step is to acknowledge emotions, rather than suppressing them, which can feel hard if you fear they may become fixed. You can lead the culture by modelling how acknowledging feelings releases them, developing cultural emotional literacy.

Self-care Second, apply self-care to get you through the short-term. What can people do together consciously? What practices can they share or lead? For instance, I have been invited to lead meditations and centring practices for teams struggling with the demands they face.

Self-disclosure Third, consider if people are constructively talking and listening with each other about worries and pressures, or are they griping and gossiping, or shutting down? Does your team have access to a coach, counsellor, therapist or trained HR specialist who can support them?

The Fork in the Road Fourth, see the setback as a fork in the road. You may not have chosen the situation, but what choices can you make to move forward? What strategies, strengths, resources and insights can you share and use? Give people buy-in on what happens next, if possible.

Articulate Values Finally, what are the over-arching values the situation gives you the opportunity to re-commit to? Are you communicating these in what you do and how you are? One leader I worked with gave a weekly call to all stakeholders during the coronavirus crisis, in which he reiterated the values of the organization: excellence, integrity and care for people. It was deeply appreciated by all.

In order, these five steps help create personal and organizational resilience. I have had the privilege of working with a group of male leaders who open conversations about vulnerability to address the high incidence of burnout, depression, substance abuse and relationship breakdown among high-level professional men for whom talking about their human struggles is often seen as weakness. Rather than oversharing for the sake of it, they know that accepting and sharing vulnerability purposefully contributes to resilience. Resilience isn't an illusory shiny surface that setbacks bounce off. Organizational resilience is built from within, with the belief that you will grow from adversity, and grow together.

DIVERSITY, INCLUSION & EMPOWERMENT

◆

We are stronger together. But this only holds true if what is together encompasses diversity and inclusion at every level. We build resilient teams, organizations and communities through building a culture that includes diverse thinking and styles.

EVIDENCE ABOUNDS that diverse teams make better decisions. Our culture needs the input of people with a range of life and work experience, perspectives and thinking styles for greater empathy and a wider range of approaches to problems. But due to our cognitive biases, we favour ideas that confirm our existing beliefs, and we favour people from our own backgrounds.

Inclusion

Increasing diversity is wasted if you don't give much attention to how unconscious norms and assumptions contribute to people feeling included or excluded.

In the experiences of some of my female-identified clients on senior leadership teams, inclusion was affected by male-identified group norms for bonding. One client told me that the men would chat about sport at the beginning of each meeting, unaware that they made little attempt to include her. I am not claiming – and neither did she – that their behaviour was wrong, but it had an effect to which they were blind.

Common Cognitive Biases

- **Affinity Bias:** we tend to prefer people like us.

- **Inter-Group Bias or 'culture fit' bias:** we tend to favour people who we perceive are part of our group, and likely to fit in with us in a comfortable way.

- **Confirmation Bias:** we will search out, interpret, focus on and remember data in a way that confirms our preconceptions.

- **Halo or Horn Effect:** we observe a positive or negative attribute of someone and use it to assess everything else about that person or thing.

- **Conformity Bias:** bias caused by group peer pressure.

- **Bias Blind Spot:** the failure to recognize your own cognitive biases.

In another example, a woman on a senior management team had to listen to men telling sexist jokes. One senior leader at a major European investment bank confessed to me that despite being asked to be the first woman on the board, the thought filled her with dread as she witnessed enough 'boy's club' behaviour to doubt she belonged – or even wanted to.

All of these leaders were tough-minded, highly competent, emotionally mature and experienced women with a great deal to offer, who found themselves frustrated in meetings.

Academic studies show that men are much more likely to interrupt, talk over and fail to give credit to a woman than a man. Several of my male clients address this unconscious behaviour, without blaming or shaming themselves, but taking responsibility to effect change in the system. Some people consciously use an 'echoing' technique, to reinforce a point a woman has made that has been ignored.

Privilege

We can't talk about diversity without addressing race. In much of Europe and North America, at the leadership level in many of our businesses and organizations, as well as in political and social spheres, the majority of people in the room are white. The norms of white privilege are invisible to all but those who are excluded from it because of the colour of their skin. In one example, a client called out a colleague who dismissed her concerns about the way she was treated by saying they didn't see colour. She was shocked to be met, not with acknowledgment, but with accusations that she was herself being racist, and felt exhausted at being asked repeatedly to justify and explain her pain.

Behaviour that encourages inclusion must be the new norm for the good of all of us. Tokenism and holding a diversity workshop isn't enough; our culture needs an ongoing commitment, and if people of colour are not in the room, there is no one to listen to. Ask rather than assume, listen, and be open to learning rather than defensive. Leadership is a life-long commitment to learning. Educate yourself by listening to and reading some of the powerful voices who are working in this area. It can be hard and painful, not least because it means sitting in the fire with our own and others' pain. But this is the deep work of thoughtful leadership for all of us.

Conscious Meetings

As conscious leaders, we bring mindful awareness to inclusiveness within group dynamics through attention to the normalized structures that support it. There is an unspoken norm to how we do meetings, for instance. The leader leads, people chime in, filling others in on progress or news from their corner of the world. The leader usually speaks most, and others falls silent when they do. They make the decisions and end the meeting. This is the invisible norm of most meetings. But a common meeting technique like brainstorming, for instance, works well for extroverts and fast thinkers, and not so much for introverts and those who like to consider their responses, rather than saying the first thing that comes to mind. This may not help access the best thinking available. Does the way you hold meetings empower individuals and realize the true potential of the group?

Empowerment comes from within, but the structures around a person can support, deny or suppress it. Here are a few suggestions, but I recommend you experiment to find what works well for you. It can feel uncomfortable to try something new and step out of your comfort zone. Old ways will try to reassert themselves, so give yourself at least two months, seek feedback and only then evaluate outcomes.

Purpose

First, be clear what your meeting is for by connecting participants to its role in the big picture of the values, purpose and vision of the group. Start the meeting here, not with the first task on the agenda. Revisit your alliance to align everyone with the values that matter to the group.

Direction of Attention

Second, notice the lines of energy and communication in the group. Do people predominantly address the leader, rather than each other? Does the leader speak most? In one of the best examples of meeting leadership I witnessed, the leader of a major arts and culture institution consciously redirected many questions aimed at her, admitting her lack of expertise, and highlighting someone at the table who might be a better source, giving them the opportunity to contribute.

In another example with a leadership team, I noticed that when one person spoke, other members of the team became excited with the ideas this triggered in them, and rushed in to express them. No one acknowledged or developed anyone else's ideas. I asked the team to notice this dynamic, and suggested that when someone next spoke and someone else wanted to respond, that the person started by acknowledging the previous speaker, and rather than steering away or blocking the first person's idea with 'but', the second speaker had to say 'and' (a technique from improvisation I also mention later when considering creativity). Within a very short time, the dynamic changed. People began talking to each other, rather than at each other. The leader could sit back and let the team work through ideas, which – given appreciation and space – developed. People felt good and creativity blossomed.

Notice Silos

Third, notice silos. They are inevitable, especially in large complex organizations, but without awareness and empathy, people disconnect from each other. When people notice they are stuck in siloed thinking, I invite them to exchange seats with the person with whom they are disagreeing. Geography is a terrific tool. We cannot see the whole picture from the chair we are sitting in. As mentioned in chapter four (see page 111), leaving an empty chair to hold the view of the wider team also brings in the bigger perspective.

Encourage Thinking

All leaders want their teams to think well. One of the most important factors in whether or not people think well is how they are being treated by other people: the quality of a person's attention determines the quality of another's thinking. Too often, we think we listen, but we don't. Agree as a group to listen, rather than interrupt. Allow someone to let you know when they are finished, as a pause may be thinking time, rather than your opportunity to jump in. Resist the urge to rush, and the impulse to correct. Acknowledge and appreciate all speakers. Spot assumptions that are limiting thinking, and ask, 'If we knew we couldn't fail, what would we do?' Rather than letting the extroverts grab the mike, go around the room, with everyone having their say. Most importantly, ask your team what they need to thrive as described on page 110 in chapter four, and empower everyone to hold accountability. If someone's impulses get the better of them, allow for understanding and empathy, at the same time as holding accountability without blame. This especially applies to the leader: you must be held to the same standards, and people need to feel safe to mention your own slip-ups. I suggest trialling these techniques in your meetings with the agreement of your group, and review the difference it makes. They may have suggestions of their own too.

Taking decisive action to encourage diversity, inclusion and empowerment is part of your leadership role. Choosing our own comfort over self- and other-awareness and avoiding hard conversations is the essence of privilege. It destroys trust and renders meaningful and lasting change less possible.

CREATIVITY & INNOVATION

Creativity and innovation are no longer the preserve of a nominated few. They are sparks to be nurtured within everyone. Often, the blocks to creativity are more emotional than mental, and thoughtful leaders understand this and skilfully shepherd this most tender, yet powerful potential in all those they lead.

WHAT GOT YOU HERE won't get you there. All leaders should have this sentence emblazoned somewhere they can see it daily. Success breeds complacency. When we believe we have the secret sauce, we repeat the formula until, of course, it fails. One leader of an organization with an esteemed history confessed to me, 'If we carry on with business-as-usual, it may feel as if the plane is flying level, but in today's environment, the reality is that it is slowly descending, and will eventually crash.'

Thoughtful leaders encourage creativity and innovation throughout, and guard against 'that's just the way we do it around here' thinking. They also take care not to bet everything on a poorly thought-through idea without calculating risk and road testing it.

Here's the problem with creativity: as individuals or groups, we try to be creator, editor and critic simultaneously. In the middle of a workshop I facilitated for a leadership team, someone had an insight: 'Why don't we feel more comfort-

able bringing "stupid" ideas to the table?' Scared of looking foolish and crippled by perfectionism, when a new idea raised its infant head, they mercilessly crushed it before it had the opportunity to breathe. As a leader, create a culture that gives space to nurture all creative ideas.

The Three Rooms Process

Creativity is often dressed in mystique, but in truth, leading it requires process rather than genius. For guidance, I'm going to turn to Walt Disney – a pioneer, not only of animation, but of codifying creative processes and embedding them into the culture of his studio. He saw the problem with creativity was not one of lack, but that the moment a creative idea broke the surface, inner and outer critics would tear it apart. So, he instituted the Three Rooms process. In this process, boundaries are held around each space of ideation, realization and critical thinking, rather than getting into all three rooms simultaneously. You can do this individually or in a group by setting a timer for each room. If you are collaborating online, you can use breakout rooms, if available.

Dreamer Room

The first room is the Dreamer Room, in which people give space to new ideas. No one blocks the new idea by saying or thinking, 'Yes, but...', rather encourages and builds with 'Yes, and...'. Powerful questions for Dreamers include:

- What part of this idea do we like best?
- If there were no limitations, what would we do?
- If we had no fear of failure, what could we dream up?
- What might be the biggest possible benefit of this idea?
- What if we took the best part and scaled it up?

Realist Room

Once you have nourished an idea, only then do you move into the Realist Room. A word of warning here: 'realist' can be confused with 'pessimist' or 'critic'. Powerful questions for the Realist Room focus on *how* to make the idea a reality:

- What resources are needed for this to work?
- What is the timeline to realize it?
- What help would we need to call in?
- How would we apply this idea in reality?
- What would the action plan look like?
- How do we evaluate it?

In the Realist Room, you re-work your Dreamer idea into something practical. Hold back from finding ways it could not be achieved, and instead focus on how it could be done.

Spoiler Room

Finally, in what Disney called the Spoiler Room, you have permission to test your more resilient idea. The questions remain open, rather than closed and directive – kicking the tyres, not slashing them:

- How do we really feel about the idea?
- What are the benefits and risks if we do, and if we don't?
- Why are we the people to do it?
- What are we ignoring?
- How does it align with our values and purpose?
- How will this look in a year's time, five years', and ten years'?

By compartmentalizing the stages, you give oxygen to the dream in the initial stages; the realist is allowed to work without the spoiler auditing; and the spoiler probes a well-thought-through idea. Ideas that survived this process were the ones that Disney would work on. When we brainstorm and in groups, we tend to fill the room with a dreamer or two, a few realists, and a lot of spoilers. In these conditions, nascent ideas don't stand a chance.

Design Thinking

The messy early stages of innovation can feel intolerable, and this stifles the confidence of people to suggest new ideas. Nobel Laureate Linus Pauling said the way to generate good ideas is to have lots of ideas and throw away the bad ones. Rather than spending huge resources in research and development behind one idea, have a few ideas that can be tested. In a method known as design thinking, ideas, products and services get developed by an agile, reiterative process of prototyping: create a 'minimum viable product' or service,

try it, measure it, learn from it, make changes and try it again. Thoughtful leadership culture has a resilient and positive attitude towards failure to encourage innovation. More people and organizations fail by never trying.

Empathy

Leaders also create the conditions for creativity and innovation by encouraging and modelling a culture with an entrepreneurial mindset in which empathy is the cornerstone. Can you empathize with the problems that you want to address and concentrate on, or are you making assumptions? This works as much for a product and service, as for a campaign or activism. How can you empathize with those who need what you are going to offer, as well as those who may resist?

For example, pioneering product designer Patricia Moore conducted empathy experiments to experience the world from the point of view of elderly people. She walked with a cane and bandaged her hands to mimic arthritis, and was shocked at how difficult it was to perform everyday tasks, such as using a can opener. Her insights resulted in the endeavour to design environments that can be accessed, understood and used to the greatest extent possible by the greatest number of people, regardless of age, size, ability or disability. Just because something has always been done in a certain way, it doesn't mean it can't be changed.

PROSPECTION

◆

Managers manage the status quo. Leaders keep one foot in the present so they can respond to what is front of them. All leadership requires management skills, but it is this visionary prospective aspect of leadership that in many ways defines it.

PSYCHOLOGISTS ATTRIBUTE MUCH of our emotional energy to the quality of the mental images we weave about the future. We are characteristically unnerved by uncertainty, and can be tempted to deny or avoid these uncomfortable feelings. We may not always be able to control the future, but leaders believe they can respond and influence creatively.

Fighting Fires

How much of your time is spent firefighting? How much time do you have to reflect and consider the future? When we take time to reflect and plan, we gather the compound cluster of our thoughts and organize them, which develops a greater sense of oversight and agency.

At times of crisis, we go into survival mode, with its stress patterns of fight, flight, freeze, fold or friend. However, the cost of this is that we create the very conditions that endanger our projects, communities and organizations by reacting and narrowing our vision, rather than seeing the big picture, envisioning opportunities, and building bridges rather than walls.

As well as practising personal centring, we need to build in organizational robustness. We can only do that as leaders if we have space to consider future-oriented questions, such as:

- What is coming that could have an effect?
- How aware and tuned-in am I?
- What can I do to be more aware of future trends?
- Although I may not know what is going to come, I know that something will, so how can I reduce our vulnerability?

These are not questions you can give time to in between emails. I recommend that every individual leader and team with whom I work, sets time aside, and holds inviolable boundaries around it, to do the work of prospection.

SUSTAINABILITY & LEGACY

How do we sustain ourselves, and our projects and organizations? How do we lead the decision-making process of today for the benefit of the leaders of the future? And ultimately, how can we lead in a way that doesn't diminish and destroy the resource upon which we all depend – the planet itself?

NATIVE AMERICAN AND FIRST NATIONS people have a profound practice of thoughtful leadership. When leaders gather to make a decision, they light and tend a fire called the Children's Fire. They consider all their decisions in the light of the Children's Fire to remind themselves of the

impact of their decisions for seven generations going forward, not just of the tribe or even humanity, but for all living beings, as well as the planet itself.

Light this fire and tend it well. Everything each of us does has an impact. For leaders, this impact needs to be conscious and long-term. Build this thoughtfulness into everything that you do. Here are three key principles:

Consider succession The aim of leadership is to produce more leaders, not more followers. An organization or project that only continues as long as one leader is involved is fragile and unsustainable. Build a culture of leadership development. Actively cultivate your successors, by spotting and developing talent rather than hoarding power and leaving succession to social Darwinism.

Think in systems and understand the interconnectedness The illusion of your separateness limits potential, creates enemies instead of allies, and is the well of unintended impact on every system on this planet. The issues we have to face at this point in history are too great, the consequences too grave, to think in terms of 'I', not 'we'.

Treat the Earth well. It was not given to you by your
parents. It was loaned to you by your children.

NATIVE AMERICAN PROVERB

MINDFULNESS EXERCISE

LOW DREAM, HIGH DREAM

❋

This is a great exercise to do with yourself, your partnership or your team to co-create and maintain a group vision. Take time out for this. You'll need two large sheets of paper and some sticky notes.

1 Decide how you want to work together with a co-created alliance.

2 On each sheet of paper draw a series of concentric circles working out from the centre, each with a label:

- For myself (if working alone)
- For the team or partnership
- For the organization
- For society and culture
- For the world

3 Write your 'Low Dream' for each of these circles on a sticky note; if other people are doing the exercise with you, each person does the same. Stick each note onto the relevant circle on the first sheet of paper (see opposite for definitions of Low and High Dreams).

4 Now do the same for a 'High Dream', but this time stick the notes onto the circles on the second sheet of paper.

5 How do you feel about the comparison? How can you turn your High Dream into reality? What would be your first step?

Think in deep time Inside a mountain in Texas, engineers working with the Long Now Foundation are building a 10,000-year clock to remind all of us of an expanded sense of time. In geological terms, we have entered the Anthropocene epoch, when human activity has the dominant effect on

climate and the environment. The prevalence of short-term thinking is a model that needs to change, and that's your leadership challenge at this point in history.

When we consider all the above, it is more urgent than ever that we transform how we do things, and that includes leadership. Hold yourself and others accountable, and demonstrate what this looks like every day with dignity. Create, articulate and enjoin others in this High Dream of leadership. A Low Dream is one we imagine if nothing changes. A High Dream is one in which we envision what we can achieve if we take on the challenges and make the greatest possible impact on the world. It is like a spell: it creates energy and purpose, unites us, and directs us onwards and upwards.

Your Leadership Commitment

Leadership is a commitment to continuous self-development. It never ends, and I hope that you are as excited for your possibilities as I am. The challenge may seem overwhelming, the vision too impossible. Do you imagine that you are different from any other leader, including the ones you admire? Remember, this is about the service you bring to the world that needs your leadership. Ask yourself these questions:

- What is my next step of leadership development?
- What can I do to start today?

I wish you all the best and look forward to living in the world that you create.

BIBLIOGRAPHY

Other resources can be found at www.fionabucklandcoaching.com

Arbinger Institute, The, *The Anatomy of Peace: How to Resolve the Heart of Conflict* (Penguin, 2016)

Brown B., *Dare to Lead: Brave Work. Tough Conversations. Whole Hearts.* (Vermilion, 2018)

Dethmer J., Chapman D. and Klemp K. W., *The 15 Commitments of Conscious Leadership* (Dethmer, Chapman & Klemp, 2015)

Hawkins P., *Leadership Team Coaching, Third Edition* (Kogan Page, 2017)

Kimsey-House H., Kimsey-House K., Sandahl P., and Whitworth L., *Co-Active Coaching, Third Edition* (Nicholas Brealey Publishing, 2011)

Kimsey-House K. and Kimsey-House H., *Co-Active Leadership: Five Ways to Lead* (Berrett-Koehler Publishers, Inc, 2015)

Kline N., *Time to Think* (Cassell, 2002)

Malandro L., *Fearless Leadership: How to Overcome Behavioral Blindspots and Transform Your Organization* (McGraw-Hill Education, 2009)

Neff K., *Self-Compassion* (Yellow Kite, 2011)

Palmer P. J., *Let Your Life Speak* (Jossey Bass, 1999)

Palmer W. and Crawford J., *Leadership Embodiment* (CreateSpace, 2013)

Rød A. and Fridjhon M., *Creating Intelligent Teams* (KR Publishing, 2016)

Rosenberg M., *Nonviolent Communication, Third Edition* (Puddle Dancer Press, 2015)

Sinek S., *Start with Why: How Great Leaders Inspire Everyone To Take Action* (Penguin, 2001)

Starhawk, *The Empowerment Manual* (New Society Publishers, 2011)

Ware B., *The Top Five Regrets of the Dying* (Hay House, 2019)

Whitelaw G. and Wetzig B., *Move to Greatness: Focusing the Four Essential Energies of a Whole and Balanced Leader* (Nicholas Brealey, 2008)

Index

ACKNOWLEDGEMENTS

I owe many of the exercises and insights in
this book to my coach training with the Co-Active
Training Institute, led by Karen and Henry Kimsey-House,
and to their masterful teachers. I also want to thank Mark
Walsh from the Embodied Facilitator Course, which has
influenced my life, leadership and coaching profoundly.
I am also grateful to the founders and teams at ORSC
(Organizational and Relational System Coaching) and
Coaching Constellations, with whom I also trained. My
gratitude to the team at Leaping Hare Press, who have been
passionate about this project. Thanks also to The School of
Life, where, as Head of Learning and a faculty member, I
have been privileged to learn and teach. Deep appreciation
to Francis Briers, Phil Askew and Maurits Kalff, who have
been a powerful influence personally and professionally,
to John Ashton and Mark Lipton, who kindly offered
feedback, and to the many friends who have
supported and encouraged me.

Finally, many thanks to past, present,
and future clients whose commitment to thoughtful
leadership renews my faith daily.

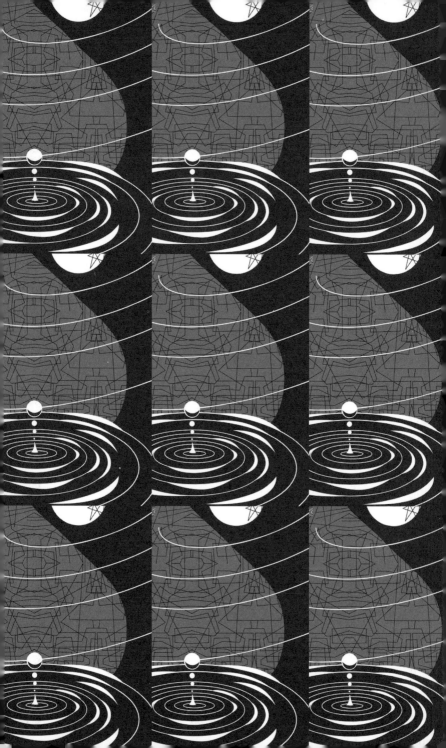